I0455959

The COMEY Senate Intelligence Committee on June 8, 2017 Testimony on Russian Interference in the 2016 Presidential Election

Edited by Richard P. Hardwood, III

©2017 FREEDOM PRESS
All Rights Reserved
No Part of this book may be reproduced,
stored in a retrieval system, or transmitted,
in any form or by any means without
written permission of the editor.

Printed in the USA
Library of Congress Cataloging in
Publication Data
ISBN-13: 978-1548101633
ISBN- 154810163X
Hardwood, Richard P, III

FAIR USE ASSERTION

Any materials used in this book to illustrate and assist in comprehension, have been used under the Fair Use Copyright assertion of Section 107

Section 107 contains a list of the various purposes for which the reproduction of a particular work may be considered fair, such as criticism, comment, news reporting, teaching, scholarship, and research. Section 107 also sets out four factors to be considered in determining whether or not a particular use is fair:

• The purpose and character of the use, including whether such use is of commercial nature or is for nonprofit educational purposes

• The nature of the copyrighted work

• The amount and substantiality of the portion used in relation to the copyrighted work as a whole

• The effect of the use upon the potential market for, or value of, the copyrighted work

The distinction between fair use and infringement may be unclear and not easily defined. There is no specific number of words, lines, or notes that may safely be taken without permission. Acknowledging the source of the copyrighted material does not substitute for obtaining permission.

The 1961 Report of the Register of Copyrights on the General Revision of the U.S. Copyright Law cites examples of activities that courts have regarded as fair use: "quotation of excerpts in a review or criticism for purposes of illustration or comment; quotation of short passages in a scholarly or technical work, for illustration or clarification of the author's observations; use in a parody of some of the content of the work parodied; summary of an address or article, with brief quotations, in a news report; reproduction by a library of a portion of a work to replace part of a damaged copy; reproduction by a teacher or student of a small part of a work to illustrate a lesson; reproduction of a work in legislative or judicial proceedings or reports; incidental and fortuitous reproduction, in a newsreel or broadcast, of a work located in the scene of an event being reported."

Copyright protects the particular way authors have expressed themselves. It does not extend to any ideas, systems, or factual information conveyed in a work.

⬚
Editor's Note:

The Senate Intelligence Committee holds a hearing on Russia's involvement in the 2016 presidential election.

Below is the full transcript from the Hearing.

Rarely do we realize we are watching history "in the making." I Believe this hearing will mark the beginning of one of the most turbulent and amazing times in our 240+ year history. When it is over everything will have changed. This transcript is compiled to allow the 'everyday man' the chance to read it without interference.

Read it...   review it...   enjoy it!

Excelsior!!

Richard P Hardwood, III

THE PLAYERS:

Mark Robert Warner (born December 15, 1954) is an American politician and the senior United States Senator from Virginia, in office since 2009. He is a member of the Democratic Party and now serves as the vice chair of both the Senate Democratic Caucus, appointed by Minority Leader Chuck Schumer, and of the Senate Intelligence Committee.

Prior to his congressional career, Warner was the 69th Governor of Virginia, holding the office from 2002–06, and is the honorary chairman of the Forward Together PAC. Warner delivered the keynote address at the 2008 Democratic National Convention. Apart from politics, Warner is also known for his involvement in telecommunications-related venture capital during the 1980s; he founded the firm Columbia Capital.

James Elroy Risch (born May 3, 1943) is an American Republican politician, rancher, and attorney from Ada County, Idaho, currently serving as the junior United States Senator from Idaho. He previously served as the 39th and 41st Lieutenant Governor (2003–2006, 2007–2009) and the 31st Governor (2006–2007) of Idaho.

Dianne Goldman Berman Feinstein born Dianne Emiel Goldman is the senior United States Senator from California. A member of the Democratic Party, she has served in the Senate since 1992. She also served as the 38th Mayor of San Francisco from 1978 to 1988.

Born in San Francisco, Feinstein graduated from Stanford University in 1955 with a B.A. in history. In the 1960s she worked in city government, and in 1970 she was elected to the San Francisco Board of Supervisors. She served as the board's first female president in 1978, during which time the assassinations of Mayor George Moscone and City Supervisor Harvey Milk drew national attention to the city. Feinstein succeeded Moscone as mayor. During her tenure as San Francisco's first female mayor she led renovation of the city's cable car system and oversaw the 1984 Democratic National Convention.

Marco Antonio Rubio (born May 28, 1971) is an American politician and attorney, and the junior United States Senator from Florida. Rubio previously served as Speaker of the Florida House of Representatives.

Rubio is a Cuban American from Miami, with degrees from the University of Florida and the University of Miami School of Law. In the late 1990s, he served as a City Commissioner for West Miami and was elected to the Florida House of Representatives in 2000, representing the 111th House district.

Ronald Lee Wyden (born May 3, 1949) is the senior United States Senator for Oregon, serving since 1996, and a member of the Democratic Party. He previously served in the United States House of Representatives from 1981 to 1996. He is the current dean of Oregon's Congressional Delegation.

Susan Margaret Collins (born December 7, 1952) is a U.S. politician who currently serves as the senior United States Senator from Maine. A member of the Republican Party,

Collins has served in the Senate since 1997, and has served as the Chairwoman of the Senate Special Committee on Aging since 2015 and previously chaired the Senate Committee on Homeland Security from 2003 to 2007. She is considered one of the most moderate Republicans in office. She also is known for her long consecutive voting streak, which reached 6,000 votes in September 2015. She is the current dean of Maine's congressional delegation.

Martin Trevor Heinrich (born October 17, 1971) is an American politician and businessman, the junior United States Senator for New Mexico, in office since 2013.

A native of Cole Camp, Missouri, Heinrich lived much of his adulthood in New Mexico, specifically Albuquerque, the state's largest city. As a member of Democratic Party, Heinrich was the U.S. Representative for New Mexico's 1st congressional district from 2009 to 2013. Heinrich won the Senate seat vacated by retiring Senator Jeff Bingaman in 2012.

Angus Stanley King Jr. (born March 31, 1944) is an American politician and attorney who is the junior United States Senator from Maine. A political independent, he served as Maine's 72nd governor from 1995 to 2003, winning his first election in a 4-way race with 35.37% of the vote.

King won Maine's 2012 Senate election to replace the retiring Republican Olympia Snowe and took office on January 3, 2013. For committee assignment purposes, he caucuses with the Democratic Party. He is the second incumbent Independent Senator, after Vermont's Bernie Sanders.

Roy Dean Blunt (born January 10, 1950) is an American politician who currently serves as the junior United States Senator from Missouri, having been in office since 2011. He is a member of the Republican Party.

Blunt served as the United States Representative from Missouri's 7th congressional district from 1997 to 2011. The district contains most of Southwest Missouri, anchored in the city of Springfield, as well as the cities of Joplin, Carthage, and Neosho, and the popular tourist destination of Branson.

Blunt served as House Majority Whip from 2003 to 2007, and was acting House Majority Leader from September 2005 to February 2006. He was the House Minority Whip during the 110th Congress starting in 2007, but after the 2008 general elections, he announced that he would step down from the position.

Blunt successfully ran for United States Senate in 2010. The following year, he was elected vice-chairman of the Senate Republican Conference. Blunt is the current dean of Missouri's Congressional Delegation.

James Paul Lankford (born March 4, 1968) is an American politician who is the junior United States Senator from Oklahoma. A member of the Republican Party, he served as the U.S. Representative for Oklahoma's 5th congressional district from 2011 to 2015.

From 1996 to 2009, Lankford was the student ministries and evangelism specialist for the Baptist General Convention of Oklahoma, and he was director of the Falls

Creek youth programming at the Falls Creek Baptist Conference Center in Davis, Oklahoma. He stepped down on September 1, 2009, to run for Congress.

In January 2014, Lankford announced he would run in the 2014 special Senate election to succeed Tom Coburn. He subsequently won the June 2014 primary with 57% of the vote, becoming the Republican nominee for the November election. He would go on to win with nearly 68% of the vote.

Joseph Manchin III (born August 24, 1947) is the senior United States Senator from West Virginia. Manchin, a member of the Democratic Party, served as the 34th Governor of West Virginia from 2005 to 2010 and the Secretary of State of West Virginia from 2001 to 2005.

Manchin has been known throughout his career to be a moderate Democrat, a fact which allowed him to hold office in West Virginia even as the state became one of the most heavily Republican in the country. He was elected governor by a large margin in 2004 and re-elected with an even larger margin 2008, even though in both years Republican presidential candidates captured the majority of West Virginia's votes. He won the special election in November 2010 to fill the seat of Senator Robert Byrd, the longest serving U.S. Senator in history, who died in office. Manchin was elected to a full term in office with 60 percent of the vote in November 2012. Manchin became the state's senior Senator when Jay Rockefeller retired in 2015.

As a senator, Manchin is known for his bipartisanship, voting or working with Republicans on issues such as abortion and gun ownership. He has opposed the energy policies of President Barack Obama, declined to vote on both the Don't Ask, Don't Tell Repeal Act of 2010 and the DREAM ACT, voted for removing federal funding from Planned Parenthood in 2015 and against in 2017, and voted to confirm most of Donald Trump's Cabinet appointees.

Thomas Bryant Cotton (born May 13, 1977) is an American politician who is the junior United States Senator from Arkansas. A member of the Republican Party, Cotton has served in the Senate since January 3, 2015. At age 40, he is currently the youngest U.S. Senator. Prior to the election of Cotton, Senator Chris Murphy from Connecticut was the youngest incumbent U.S. Senator, as he was 39 when first elected in 2012.

Cotton was first elected to the Senate in 2014, defeating two-term Democratic incumbent Mark Pryor. He previously served one term in the United States House of Representatives from 2013 until 2015.

Kamala Devi Harris (born October 20, 1964) is an American attorney and politician who is the junior United States Senator from California. She is a member of the Democratic Party and served as the 32nd Attorney General of California.

Harris graduated from Howard University and University of California, Hastings College of the Law. She worked as a Deputy District Attorney in Alameda County, California (1990–98). She served as Managing Attorney of the Career Criminal Unit in the San Francisco District Attorney's Office (1998-2000) and as Chief of the Community and

Neighborhood Division in the office of San Francisco City Attorney (2000–03). In 2003, she was elected as California's first African American female District Attorney of San Francisco, defeating incumbent Terence Hallinan. She was re-elected in 2007 and served from 2004 to 2011.

John Cornyn III (born February 2, 1952) is an American politician, lawyer and the senior United States Senator from Texas, serving since 2002. He is a member of the Republican Party and the current Senate Majority Whip for the 115th Congress. Cornyn previously served as Chairman of the National Republican Senatorial Committee from 2007 to 2011.

Born in Houston, Cornyn is a graduate from Trinity University and St. Mary's University School of Law, receiving his LL.M. from the University of Virginia School of Law. Cornyn was a Judge on Texas' 37th District Court from 1985 to 1991, until he was elected an associate justice of the Texas Supreme Court, where he served 1991 to 1997. In 1998, Cornyn was elected Attorney General of Texas, serving one term until winning a seat in the U.S. Senate in 2002. He was re-elected to a second term in 2008 and to a third term in 2014.

John Francis "Jack" Reed (born November 12, 1949), is the senior United States Senator from Rhode Island, serving since 1997. A member of the Democratic Party, he previously served in the United States House of Representatives for Rhode Island's 2nd congressional district from 1991 to 1997

John Sidney McCain III (born August 29, 1936) is an American politician who currently serves as the senior

United States Senator from Arizona. He was the Republican nominee for the 2008 U.S. presidential election.

Testimony

James B. Comey, the former F.B.I. director who was fired
by President Trump, appeared in front of the Senate
Intelligence Committee on Thursday, June 8, 2017.

BURR: I'd like to call this hearing to order.

Director Comey, I appreciate your willingness to appear
before the committee today, and more importantly, I
thank you for your dedicated service and leadership to the
Federal Bureau of Investigation. Your appearance today
speaks to the trust we have built over the years, and I'm
looking forward to a very open and candid discussion
today.

BURR: I'd like to remind my colleagues that we will
reconvene in closed session at 1 PM today and I ask that
you reserve for that venue any questions that might get
into classified information. The director has been very
gracious with his time, but the vice chairman and I have
worked out a very specific timeline for his commitment to
be on the Hill, so we will do everything we can to meet
that agreement.

The Senate Select Committee on Intelligence exists to
certify for the other 85 members of the United States
Senate and the American people that the intelligence
community is operating lawfully and has the necessary
authorities and tools to accomplish its mission and keep
America safe. Part of our mission, beyond the oversight we
continue to provide to the intelligence community and its
activities, is to investigate Russian interference in the 2016
U.S. elections. The committee's work continues. This
hearing represents part of that effort.

1   Jim, allegations have been swirling in the press for the last
2   several weeks, and today's your opportunity to set the
3   record straight. Yesterday, I read with interest your
4   statement for the record. And I think it provides some
5   helpful details surrounding your interactions with the
6   president.
7
8   It clearly lays out your understanding of those discussions,
9   actions you took following each conversation and your
10 state of mind. I very much appreciate your candor, and I
11 think it's helpful as we work through to determine the
12 ultimate truth behind possible Russian interference in the
13 2016 elections.
14
15 Your statement also provides texture and context to your
16 interactions with the president, from your vantage point,
17 and outlines a strained relationship. The American people
18 need to hear your side of the story just as they need to
19 hear the president's descriptions of events.
20
21 These interactions also highlight the importance of the
22 committee's ongoing investigation. Our experienced staff
23 is interviewing all relevant parties and some of the most
24 sensitive intelligence in our country's possession.
25
26 We will establish the facts, separate from rampant
27 speculation, and lay them out for the American people to
28 make their own judgment. Only then will we as a nation be
29 able to move forward and to put this episode to rest.
30 There are several outstanding issues not addressed in your
31 statement that I hope you'll clear up for the American
32 people today. Did the president's request for loyalty —
33 your impression that — that the one-on-one dinner of
34 January 27th was, and I quote, "at least in part an effort to

create some sort of patronage relationship," or his March 30th phone call asking what you could do to lift the cloud of Russia investigation in any way, alter your approach of the FBI's investigation into General Flynn or the broader investigation into Russia and possible links to the campaign?

In your opinion, did potential Russian efforts to establish links with individuals in the Trump orbit rise to the level we could define as collusion? Or was it a counterintelligence concern?

There's been a significant public speculation about your decision-making related to the Clinton e-mail investigation. Why did you decide publicly — to publicly announce FBI's recommendations that the Department of Justice not pursue criminal charges? You have described it as a choice between a bad decision and a worse decision. The American people need to understand the facts behind your action.

This committee is uniquely suited to investigate Russia's interference in the 2016 elections. We also have a unified, bipartisan approach to what is a highly charged partisan issue. Russian activities during 2016 election may have been aimed at one party's candidate, but as my colleague, Senator Rubio, says frequently, in 2018 and 2020, it could be aimed at anyone, at home or abroad.

My colleague, Senator Warner, and I have worked in — have worked to to stay in lockstep on this investigation. We've had our differences on approach at times. But I've constantly stressed that we need to be a team. And I think Senator Warner agrees with me.

1
2 We must keep these questions above politics and
3 partisanship. It's too important to be tainted by anyone
4 trying to score political points.
5
6 With that, again, I welcome you, Director.
7
8 And I turn to the vice chairman for any comments he
9 might have.
10
11 **WARNER:** Well, thank you, Mr. Chairman.
12
13 And let me start by, again, absolutely (sic) thanking all the
14 members of the committee for the seriousness in which
15 they've taken on this task.
16
17 **WARNER:** Mr. Comey, thank you for agreeing to come
18 testify as part of this committee's investigation into Russia.
19 I realize that this hearing has been, obviously, the focus of
20 a lot of Washington in the last few days. But the truth is
21 many Americans who may be tuning in today probably
22 haven't focused on every twist and turn of the
23 investigation.
24
25 So I'd like to briefly describe, at least from this senator's
26 standpoint, what we already know and what we're still
27 investigating. To be clear, this whole (sic) investigation is
28 not about relitigating the election. It's not about who won
29 or lost. And it sure as heck is not about Democrats versus
30 Republicans.
31
32 We're here because a foreign adversary attacked us right
33 here at home, plain and simple, not by guns or missiles,

1   but by foreign operatives seeking to hijack our most
2   important democratic process — our presidential election.
3
4   Russian spies engaged in a series of online cyber raids and
5   a broad campaign of disinformation, all ultimately aimed
6   at sowing chaos to us to undermine public faith in our
7   process, in our leadership and ultimately in ourselves.
8
9   And that's not just this senator's opinion, it is the
10 unanimous determination of the entire U.S. intelligence
11 community. So we must find out the full story, what the
12 Russians did, and, candidly, as some other colleagues have
13 mentioned, why they were so successful. And, more
14 importantly, we must determine the necessary steps to
15 take to protect our democracy and ensure they can't do it
16 again.
17
18 Chairman mentioned elections in 2018 and 2020. In my
19 home state of Virginia, we have elections this year, in
20 2017. Simply put, we cannot let anything or anyone
21 prevent us from getting to the bottom of this.
22
23 Now, Mr. Comey, let me say at the outset we haven't
24 always agreed on every issue. In fact, I've occasionally
25 questioned some of the actions you've taken. But I've
26 never had any reason to question your integrity, your
27 expertise or your intelligence.
28
29 You've been a straight shooter with this committee, and
30 have been willing to speak truth to power, even at the risk
31 of your own career, which makes the way in which you
32 were fired by the president ultimately shocking.
33

1 **WARNER:** Recall, we began this entire process with the
2 president and his staff first denying that the Russians were
3 ever involved, and then falsely claiming that no one from
4 his team was never in touch with any Russians.
5
6 We know that's just not the truth. Numerous Trump
7 associates had undisclosed contacts with Russians before
8 and after the election, including the president's attorney
9 general, his former national security adviser and his
10 current senior adviser, Mr. Kushner.
11
12 That doesn't even begin to count the host of additional
13 campaign associates and advisers who've also been caught
14 up in this massive web. We saw Mr. Trump's campaign
15 manager, Mr. Manafort, forced to step down over ties to
16 Russian-backed entities. The national security adviser,
17 General Flynn, had to resign over his lies about
18 engagements with the Russians.
19
20 And we saw the candidate him — himself, express an odd
21 and unexplained affection for the Russian dictator, while
22 calling for the hacking of his opponent. There's a lot to
23 investigate. Enough, in fact that then Director Comey
24 publicly acknowledged that he was leading an
25 investigation into those links between Mr. Trump's
26 campaign and the Russian government.
27
28 As the director of the FBI, Mr. Comey was ultimately
29 responsible for conducting that investigation, which might
30 explain why you're sitting now as a private citizen.
31
32 What we didn't know was, at the same time that this
33 investigation was proceeding, the president himself
34 appears to have been engaged in an effort to influence, or

at least co-opt, the director of the FBI. The testimony that Mr. Comey has submitted for today's hearing is very disturbing.

For example, on January 27th, after summoning Director Comey to dinner, the president appears to have threatened the (sic) director's job while telling him, quote, "I need loyalty. I expect loyalty."

WARNER: At a later meeting, on February 14th, the president asked the attorney general to leave the Oval Office so that he could privately ask Director Comey, again, quote, "to see way clear (sic) to letting Flynn go."

That is a statement that Director Comey interpreted as a — as a request that he drop the investigation, connected to General Flynn's false statements. Think about it: the president of the United States asking the FBI director to drop an ongoing investigation.

And, after that, the president called the FBI director on two additional occasions, March 30th and April 11th, and asked him again, quote, "to lift the cloud" on the Russian investigation.

Now, Director Comey denied each of these improper requests. The loyalty pledge, the admonition to drop the Flynn investigation, the request to lift the cloud on the Russia investigation. Of course, after his refusals, Director Comey was fired.

The initial explanation for the firing didn't pass any smell test. So now Director Comey was fired because (sic) he didn't treat Hillary Clinton appropriately. Of course, that

1 explanation lasted about a day, because the president
2 himself then made very clear that he was thinking about
3 Russia when he decided to fire Director Comey.
4
5 Shockingly, reports suggest that the president admitted as
6 much in an Oval Office meeting with the Russians the day
7 after Director Comey was fired, disparaging our country's
8 top law enforcement official as a, quote/unquote, "nut
9 job." The president allegedly suggested that his firing
10 relieved great pressure on his feelings about Russia.
11
12 This is not happening in isolation. At the same time the
13 president was engaged in these efforts with Director
14 Comey, he was also, at least allegedly, asking senior
15 leaders of the intelligence community to downplay the
16 Russia investigation or to intervene with the director.
17
18 Yesterday, we had DNI Director Coats and NSA Director
19 Admiral Rogers, who were offered a number of
20 opportunities to flatly deny those press reports. They
21 expressed their opinions, but they did not take that
22 opportunity to deny those reports. They did not take
23 advantage of that opportunity. In my belief, that's not how
24 the president of the United States should behave.
25
26 Regardless of the outcome of our investigation into the
27 Russia links, Director Comey's firing and his testimony
28 raise separate and troubling questions that we must get to
29 the bottom of.
30
31 Again, as I said at the outset, I've seen firsthand how
32 seriously every member of this committee is taking his
33 work. I'm proud of the committee's efforts so far. Let me
34 be clear: This is not a witch hunt. This is not fake news. It is

1 an effort to protect our country from a new threat that,
2 quite honestly, will not go away any time soon.
3
4 So, Mr. Comey, your testimony here today will help us
5 move towards that goal. I look forward to that testimony.
6
7 **WARNER:** Thank you, Mr. Chairman.
8
9 **BURR:** Thank you, Vice Chairman.
10
11 Director, as discussed, when you agreed to appear before
12 the committee, it would be under oath. I'd ask you to
13 please stand. Raise your right hand. Do you solemnly
14 swear to tell the truth, the whole truth, and nothing but
15 the truth, so help you God?
16
17 **COMEY:** (OFF-MIKE)
18
19 **BURR:** Please be seated.
20
21 Director Comey, you're now under oath.
22
23 And I would just note to members, you will be recognized
24 by seniority for a period up to seven minutes. And again, it
25 is the intent to move to a closed session no later than 1
26 p.m.
27
28 With that, Director Comey, you are recognized. You have
29 the floor for as long as you might need.
30
31 Thank you, Mr. Chairman. Ranking Member Warner,
32 members of the committee, thank you for inviting me here
33 to testify today. I've submitted my statement for the
34 record and I'm not going to repeat it here this morning. I

1 thought I would just offer some very brief introductory
2 remarks and then I would welcome your questions.
3
4 When I was appointed FBI director in 2013, I understood
5 that I served at the pleasure of the president. Even though
6 I was appointed to a 10 year term, which Congress created
7 in order to underscore the importance of the FBI being
8 outside of politics and independent, I understood that I
9 could be fired by a president for any reason, or for no
10 reason at all.
11
12 And on May the 9th, when I learned that I had been fired,
13 for that reason, I immediately came home as a private
14 citizen. But then, the explanations — the shifting
15 explanations, confused me and increasingly concerned me.
16
17 **COMEY:** They confused me because the president and I
18 had had multiple conversations about my job, both before
19 and after he took office. And he had repeatedly told me I
20 was doing a great job and he hoped I would stay. And I had
21 repeatedly assured him that I did intend to stay and serve
22 out the remaining six years of my term.
23
24 He told me repeatedly that he had talked to lots of people
25 about me, including our current attorney general, and had
26 learned that I was doing a great job and that I was
27 extremely well-liked by the FBI workforce.
28
29 So it confused me when I saw on television the president
30 saying that he actually fired me because of the Russia
31 investigation and learned, again, from the media that he
32 was telling, privately, other parties that my firing had
33 relieved great pressure on the Russia investigation.
34

1 I was also confused by the initial explanation that was
2 offered publicly, that I was fired because of the decisions I
3 had made during the election year. That didn't make sense
4 to me for a whole bunch of reasons, including the time and
5 all the water that had gone under the bridge since those
6 hard decisions that had to be made. That didn't make any
7 sense to me.
8
9 And although the law required no reason at all to fire an
10 FBI director, the administration then chose to defame me
11 and, more importantly, the FBI by saying that the
12 organization was in disarray, that it was poorly led, that
13 the workforce had lost confidence in its leader.
14
15 Those were lies, plain and simple, and I am so sorry that
16 the FBI workforce had to hear them and I'm so sorry that
17 the American people were told them.
18
19 I worked every day at the FBI to help make that great
20 organization better. And I say "help" because I did nothing
21 alone at the FBI. There are no indispensable people at the
22 FBI. The organization's great strength is that its values and
23 abilities run deep and wide.
24
25 The FBI will be fine without me. The FBI's mission will be
26 relentlessly pursued by its people, and that mission is to
27 protect the American people and uphold the Constitution
28 of the United States.
29
30 **COMEY:** I will deeply miss being part of that mission, but
31 this organization and its mission will go on long beyond me
32 and long beyond any particular administration.
33

1 I have a message before I close for the — my former
2 colleagues at the FBI. But first, I want the American people
3 to know this truth: The FBI is honest. The FBI is strong. And
4 the FBI is, and always will be, independent.
5
6 And now to my former colleagues, if I may. I am so sorry
7 that I didn't get the chance to say goodbye to you
8 properly. It was the honor of my life to serve beside you,
9 to be part of the FBI family. And I will miss it for the rest of
10 my life.
11
12 Thank you for standing watch. Thank you for doing so
13 much good for this country. Do that good as long as ever
14 you can.
15
16 And, Senators, I look forward to your questions.
17
18 **BURR:** Director, thank you for that testimony, both oral
19 and the written testimony that you provided to the
20 committee yesterday and made public to the American
21 people.
22
23 The chair would recognize himself, first, for 12 minutes,
24 vice chair for 12 minutes, based upon the agreement we
25 have.
26
27 Director, did the Special Counsel's Office review and/or
28 edit your written testimony?
29
30 **COMEY:** No.
31
32 **BURR:** Do you have any doubt that Russia attempted to
33 interfere in the 2016 elections?
34

COMEY: None.

BURR: Do you have any doubt that the Russian government was behind the intrusions in the DNC and the DCCC systems, and the subsequent leaks of that information?

COMEY: No, no doubt.

BURR: Do you have any doubt that the Russian government was behind the cyber intrusion in the state voter files?

COMEY: No.

BURR: Do you have any doubt that officials of the Russian government were fully aware of these activities?

COMEY: No doubt.

BURR: Are you confident that no votes cast in the 2016 presidential election were altered?

COMEY: I'm confident. By the time — when I left as director, I had seen no indication of that whatsoever.

BURR: Director Comey, did the president at any time ask you to stop the FBI investigation into Russian involvement in the 2016 U.S. elections?

COMEY: Not to my understanding, no.

1 **BURR:** Did any individual working for this administration,
2 including the Justice Department, ask you to stop the
3 Russian investigation?
4
5 **COMEY:** No.
6
7 **BURR:** Director, when the president requested that you,
8 and I quote, "let Flynn go," General Flynn had an
9 unreported contact with the Russians, which is an offense.
10 And if press accounts are right, there might have been
11 discrepancies between facts and his FBI testimony.
12
13 In your estimation, was General Flynn, at that time, in
14 serious legal jeopardy? And in addition to that, do you
15 sense that the president was trying to obstruct justice, or
16 just seek for a way for Mike Flynn to save face, given he
17 had already been fired?
18
19 **COMEY:** General Flynn, at that point in time, was in legal
20 jeopardy. There was an open FBI criminal investigation of
21 his statements in connection with the Russian contacts
22 and the contacts themselves. And so that was my
23 assessment at the time.
24
25 I don't think it's for me to say whether the conversation I
26 had with the president was an effort to obstruct. I took it
27 as a very disturbing thing, very concerning, but that's a
28 conclusion I'm sure the special counsel will work towards,
29 to try and understand what the intention was there, and
30 whether that's an offense.
31
32 **BURR:** Director, is it possible that, as part of this FBI
33 investigation, the FBI could find evidence of criminality

1 that is not tied to — to the 2016 elections — possible
2 collusion or coordination with Russians?
3
4 **COMEY:** Sure.
5
6 **BURR:** So there could be something that just fits a criminal
7 aspect to this that doesn't have anything to do with the
8 2016 election cycle?
9
10
11 **COMEY:** Correct. In any complex investigation, when you
12 start turning over rocks, sometimes you find things that
13 are unrelated to the primary investigation, that are
14 criminal in nature.
15
16 **BURR:** Director Comey, you have been criticized publicly
17 for the decision to present your findings on the e-mail
18 investigation directly to the American people. Have you
19 learned anything since that time that would've changed
20 what you said, or how you chose to inform the American
21 people?
22
23 **COMEY:** Honestly, no. I mean, it caused a whole lot of
24 personal pain for me, but, as I look back, given what I
25 knew at the time and even what I've learned since, I think
26 it was the best way to try and protect the justice
27 institution, including the FBI.
28
29 **BURR:** In the public domain is this question of the Steele
30 dossier, a document that has been around, now, for over a
31 year. I'm not sure when the FBI first took possession of it,
32 but the media had it before you had it and we had it.
33

1 At the time of your departure from the FBI, was the FBI
2 able to confirm any criminal allegations contained in the
3 Steele document?
4
5 **COMEY:** Mr. Chairman, I don't think that's a question I can
6 answer in an open setting because it goes into the details
7 of the investigation.
8
9 **BURR:** Director, the term we hear most often is
10 "collusion." When people are describing possible links
11 between Americans and Russian government entities
12 related to the interference in our election, would you say
13 that it's normal for foreign governments to reach out to
14 members of an incoming administration?
15
16 **COMEY:** Yes.
17
18 **BURR:** At what point does the normal contact cross the
19 line into an attempt to recruit agents or influence (sic) or
20 spies?
21
22 **COMEY:** Difficult to say in the abstract. It depends upon
23 the context, whether there's an effort to keep it covert,
24 what the nature of the requests made of the American by
25 the foreign government are. It's a — it's a judgment call
26 based on a whole lot of facts.
27
28 **BURR:** At what point would that recruitment become a
29 counterintelligence threat to our country?
30
31 **COMEY:** Again, difficult to answer in the abstract. But
32 when — when a foreign power is using especially coercion
33 or some sort of pressure to try and co-opt an American,
34 especially a government official, to act on its behalf, that's

1   a serious concern to the FBI and at the heart of the FBI's
2   counterintelligence mission.
3
4   **BURR:** So if you've got a — a — a 36-page document of —
5   of specific claims that are out there, the FBI would have to,
6   for counterintelligence reasons, try to verify anything that
7   might be claimed in there. One, and probably first and
8   foremost, is the counterintelligence concerns that we have
9   about blackmail. Would that be an accurate statement?
10
11   **COMEY:** Yes. If the FBI receives a credible allegation that
12   there is some effort to co-opt, coerce, direct, employ
13   covertly an American on behalf of the foreign power,
14   that's the basis on which a counterintelligence
15   investigation is opened.
16
17   **BURR:** And when you read the dossier, what was your
18   reaction, given that it was 100 percent directed at the
19   president-elect?
20
21   **COMEY:** Not a question I can answer in an open setting,
22   Mr. Chairman.
23
24   **BURR:** OK. When did you become aware of the cyber
25   intrusion?
26
27   **COMEY:** The first cyber — it was all kinds of cyber
28   intrusions going on all the time. The first Russia-connected
29   cyber intrusion, I became aware of in the late summer of
30   2015.
31
32   **BURR:** And in that timeframe, there were more than the
33   DNC and the DCCC that were targets.
34

1 **COMEY:** Correct. There was a massive effort to target
2 government and nongovernmental — near-governmental
3 agencies like nonprofits.
4
5 **BURR:** What would be the estimate of how many entities
6 out there the Russians specifically targeted in that
7 timeframe?
8
9 **COMEY:** It's hundreds. I suppose it could be more than
10 1,000, but it's at least hundreds.
11
12 **BURR:** When did you become aware that data had been
13 exfiltrated?
14
15   **COMEY:** I'm not sure, exactly. I think either late '15 or
16 early '16.
17
18 **BURR:** And did — did you, the director of the FBI, have
19 conversations with the last administration about the risk
20 that this posed?
21
22 **COMEY:** Yes.
23
24 **BURR:** And share with us, if you will, what actions they
25 took.
26
27 **COMEY:** Well, the FBI had already undertaken an effort to
28 notify all the victims — and that's what we consider the
29 entities that were attacked as part of this massive spear
30 phishing campaign. And so we notified them in an effort to
31 disrupt what might be ongoing.
32
33 Then there was a series of continuing interactions with
34 entities through the rest of '15 into '16, and then,

1 throughout '16, the administration was trying to decide
2 how to respond to the intrusion activity that it saw.
3
4 **BURR:** And the FBI, in this case, unlike other cases that you
5 might investigate — did you ever have access to the actual
6 hardware that was hacked? Or did you have to rely on a
7 third party to provide you the data that they had
8 collected?
9
10 **COMEY:** In the case of the DNC, and, I believe, the DCCC,
11 but I'm sure the DNC, we did not have access to the
12 devices themselves. We got relevant forensic information
13 from a private party, a high-class entity, that had done the
14 work. But we didn't get direct access.
15
16 **BURR:** But no content?
17
18 **COMEY:** Correct.
19
20 **BURR:** Isn't content an important part of the forensics
21 from a counterintelligence standpoint?
22
23 **COMEY:** It is, although what was briefed to me by my folks
24 — the people who were my folks at the time is that they
25 had gotten the information from the private party that
26 they needed to understand the intrusion by the spring of
27 2016.
28
29 **BURR:** Let me go back, if I can, very briefly, to the decision
30 to publicly go out with your results on the e-mail.
31
32 Was your decision influenced by the attorney general's
33 tarmac meeting with the former president, Bill Clinton?
34

1 **COMEY:** Yes. In — in an ultimately conclusive way, that
2 was the thing that capped it for me, that I had to do
3 something separately to protect the credibility of the
4 investigation, which meant both the FBI and the Justice
5 Department.
6
7 **BURR:** Were there other things that contributed to that
8 that you can describe in an open session?
9
10 **COMEY:** There were other things that contributed to that.
11 One significant item I can't, I know the committee's been
12 briefed on. There's been some public accounts of it, which
13 are nonsense, but I understand the committee's been
14 briefed on the classified facts.
15
16 Probably the only other consideration that I guess I can
17 talk about in an open setting is, at one point, the attorney
18 general had directed me not to call it an investigation, but
19 instead to call it a matter, which confused me and
20 concerned me.
21
22 But that was one of the bricks in the load that led me to
23 conclude, I have to step away from the department if
24 we're to close this case credibly.
25
26 **BURR:** Director, my last question: You're not only a
27 seasoned prosecutor, you've led the FBI for years. You
28 understand the investigative process. You've worked with
29 this committee closely, and we're grateful to you because I
30 think we've — we've mutually built trust in what your
31 organization does and — and what we do.
32
33 Is there any doubt in your mind that this committee can
34 carry out its oversight role in the 2016 Russian

1 involvement in the elections in parallel with the — now —
2 special counsel that's been set up?

3

4 **COMEY:** No — no doubt. It can be done. It requires lots of
5 conversations, but Bob Mueller is one of this country's
6 great, great pros. And I'm sure you all will be able to work
7 it out with him to run it in parallel.

8

9 **BURR:** I want to thank you once again, and I want to turn
10 to the vice chairman.

11

12 **WARNER:** Thank you, Mr. Chairman. And, again, Director
13 Comey, thank you for your service.

14

15 And your comments to your FBI family, I know, were
16 heartfelt. Know that, even though there are some in the
17 administration who've tried to smear your reputation, you
18 had Acting Director McCabe, in public testimony a few
19 weeks back and in public testimony yesterday, reaffirm
20 that the vast majority of the (sic) FBI community had great
21 trust in your leadership and, obviously, trust in your
22 integrity.

23

24 I want to go through a number of the meetings that you
25 referenced in your testimony. And let's start with the
26 January 6th meeting in Trump Tower, where you went up
27 with a series of officials to brief the president-elect on the
28 Russia investigation. My understanding is you remained
29 afterwards to brief him on, again, quote, "some personally
30 sensitive aspects" of the information you relayed.

31

32 Now, you said, after that briefing, you felt compelled to
33 document that conversation, that you actually started
34 documenting it soon as you got into the car.

1
2 Now, you've had extensive experience at the Department
3 of Justice and at the FBI. You've worked under presidents
4 of both parties. What was it about that meeting that led
5 you to determine that you needed to start putting down a
6 written record?
7
8 **COMEY:** A combination of things, I think — the
9 circumstances, the subject matter and the person I was
10 interacting with. Circumstances first: I was alone with the
11 president of the United States — or the president-elect,
12 soon to be president.
13
14 The subject matter: I was talking about matters that touch
15 on the FBI's core responsibility and that relate to the
16 president — president-elect personally.
17
18 And then the nature of the person: I was honestly
19 concerned that he might lie about the nature of our
20 meeting, and so I thought it really important to document.
21
22 That combination of things, I'd never experienced before,
23 but it led me to believe I've got to write it down, and I've
24 got to write it down in a very detailed way.
25
26 **WARNER:** I think that's a very important statement you
27 just made. And my understanding is that then, again,
28 unlike your dealings with presidents of either parties in
29 your past experience, in every subsequent meeting or
30 conversation with this president, you created a written
31 record.
32

1   Did you feel that you needed to create this written record
2   or (sic) these memos because they might need to be relied
3   on at some future date?
4
5   **COMEY:** Sure. I created records after conversations, and I
6   think I did it after each of our nine conversations. If I
7   didn't, I did it for nearly all of them, especially the ones
8   that were substantive.
9
10 I knew that there might come a day when I would need a
11 record of what had happened, not just to defend myself,
12 but to defend the FBI and — and our integrity as an
13 institution and the independence of our investigative
14 function. That's what made this so — so difficult, is it was
15 a combination of circumstances, subject matter, and the
16 particular person.
17
18 **WARNER:** And so, in all your experience, this was the only
19 president that you felt like, in every meeting, you needed
20 to document, because at some point, using your words, he
21 might put out a non-truthful representation of that
22 meeting?
23
24 Now...
25
26 **(CROSSTALK)**
27
28 **COMEY:** That's right, Senator.
29
30 And I — I — as I said in my written testimony, as FBI
31 director, I interacted with President Obama. I spoke only
32 twice in three years, and didn't document it. When I was
33 deputy attorney general, I had one one-on-one meeting

1 with President Bush about a very important and difficult
2 national security matter.
3
4 I didn't write a memo documenting that conversation
5 either — sent a quick e-mail to my staff to let them know
6 there was something going on, but I didn't feel, with
7 President Bush, the need to document it in that way, again
8 (sic), because of — the combination of those factors just
9 wasn't present with either President Bush or President
10 Obama.
11
12 **WARNER:** I — I think that is very significant. I think others
13 will probably question that.
14
15 Now, our chairman and I have requested those memos. It
16 is our hope that the FBI will get this committee access to
17 those memos so that, again, we can read that
18 contemporaneous rendition, so that we've got your side of
19 the story.
20
21 Now, I know members have said, and press has said, that if
22 you were — a great deal's been made of whether the
23 president — you were asked to, in effect, indicate whether
24 the president was the subject of any investigation.
25
26 And my understanding is, prior to your meeting on January
27 6th, you discussed with your leadership team whether or
28 not you should be prepared to assure then President-Elect
29 Trump that the FBI was not investigating him personally.
30
31 Now, my understanding is your leadership team agreed
32 with that. But was that a unanimous decision? Was there
33 any debate about that?
34

1 **COMEY:** Was it unanimous? One of the members of the
2 leadership team had a view that, although it was
3 technically true, we did not have a counterintelligence file
4 case open on then-President-elect Trump.
5
6 His concern was, because we're looking at the potential —
7 again, that's the subject of the investigation —
8 coordination between the campaign and Russia, because it
9 was President Trump — President-elect Trump's
10 campaign, this person's view was, inevitably, his behavior,
11 his conduct will fall within the scope of that work.
12
13 And so he was reluctant to make the statement that I
14 made. I disagreed. I thought it was fair to say what was
15 literally true: There is not a counterintelligence
16 investigation of Mr. Trump. And I decided, in the moment,
17 to say it, given the nature of our conversation.
18
19 **WARNER:** At that moment in time, did you ever revisit that
20 as a — in — in these subsequent sessions?
21
22 **COMEY:** With the FBI leadership team?
23
24 **WARNER:** With the team — with your (sic) team.
25
26 **COMEY:** Sure, and — and the — the leader who had that
27 view — it didn't change. His view was still that it was
28 probably — although literally true, his concern was it could
29 be misleading, because the nature of the investigation was
30 such that it might well touch — obviously, it would touch
31 the campaign, and the person at the head of the campaign
32 would be the candidate. And so that was his view
33 throughout.
34

1 **WARNER:** Let me move to the January 27th dinner, where
2 you said, quote, "The president began by asking me
3 whether I wanted to stay on as FBI director. He also
4 indicated that lots of people" — again, your words —
5 "wanted the job."
6
7 You go on to say that the dinner itself was seemingly an
8 effort to, quote, "have you ask him for your job," and
9 create some sort of, quote/unquote, "patronage
10 relationship."
11
12 The president's (sic) — seems, from my reading of your
13 memo, to be holding your job, or your possibility of
14 continuing in your job, over your head in a fairly direct
15 way. What was your impression, and what did you mean
16 by this notion of a patronage relationship?
17
18 **COMEY:** Well, my impression — and, again, it's my
19 impression. I could always be wrong. But my common
20 sense told me that what was going on is either he had
21 concluded, or someone had told him, that you didn't —
22 you've already asked Comey to stay, and you didn't get
23 anything for it, and that the dinner was an effort to build a
24 relationship — in fact, he asked specifically — of loyalty in
25 the context of asking me to stay.
26
27 And, as I said, what was odd about that is we'd already
28 talked twice about it by that point. And he'd said, I very
29 much hope you'll stay, I hope you'll stay.
30
31 In fact, I just remembered, sitting here, a third one. When
32 — you've seen the picture of me walking across the Blue
33 Room. And what the president whispered in my ear was, "I

1 really look forward to working with you." So, after those
2 encounters...
3
4 **WARNER:** And that was just a few days before you were
5 fired.
6
7 **COMEY:** ... yeah, that was on the 20 — the Sunday after
8 the inauguration.
9
10 The next Friday, I have dinner, and the president begins by
11 wanting to talk about my job. And so I'm sitting there,
12 thinking, wait a minute, three times, we've already —
13 you've already asked me to stay, or talked about me
14 staying.
15
16 **COMEY:** And my common sense — again, I could be
17 wrong, but my common sense told me what's going on
18 here is that he's looking to get something in exchange for
19 granting my request to stay in the job.
20
21 **WARNER:** And again, we all understand — I was a
22 governor, I had people work for me. But this constant
23 request — and, again, quoting you, him saying that he —
24 despite you explaining your independence, he kept coming
25 back to "I need loyalty." "I expect loyalty."
26
27 Had you ever had any of those kind of requests before,
28 from anyone else you'd worked for in the government?
29
30 **COMEY:** No, and what made me uneasy was I'm, at that
31 point, the director of the FBI. The reason that Congress
32 created a ten-year term is so that the director is not
33 feeling as if they're serving at — with political loyalty owed
34 to any particular person.

1
2 The — the statue of Justice has a blindfold on because
3 you're not supposed to be peeking out to see whether
4 your patron is pleased or not with what you're doing.
5
6 It should be about the facts and the law. That's why I was
7 — that's why I became FBI director: to be in that kind of
8 position. So that's why I was so uneasy.
9
10 **WARNER:** Well, let me — let me move on. My time's
11 running out. February 14th — again, it seems a bit strange.
12 You were in a meeting. And your direct superior, the
13 attorney general, was in that meeting, as well.
14
15 Yet the president asked everyone to leave, including the
16 attorney general — to leave, before he brought up the
17 matter of General Flynn. What was your impression of that
18 type of action? Had you ever seen anything like that
19 before?
20
21 **COMEY:** No. My impression was, something big is about to
22 happen. I need to remember every single word that is
23 spoken. And, again, I could be wrong, but I'm 56 years old.
24 I've been — seen a few things.
25
26 My sense was the attorney general knew he shouldn't be
27 leaving, which is why he was lingering. And I don't know
28 Mr. Kushner well, but I think he picked up on the same
29 thing. And so I knew something was about to happen that I
30 needed to pay very close attention to.
31
32 **WARNER:** And I — I found it very interesting that, in the
33 memo that you wrote after this February 14th pull-aside,

1 you made clear that you wrote that memo in a way that
2 was unclassified.
3
4 If you affirmatively made the decision to write a memo
5 that was unclassified, was that because you felt, at some
6 point, the facts of that meeting would have to come clean
7 and come clear and actually be able to be cleared in a way
8 that could be shared with the American people?
9
10 **COMEY:** Well, I remember thinking, this is a very
11 disturbing development, really important to our work. I
12 need to document it and preserve it in a way — and — and
13 this committee gets this, but sometimes when things are
14 classified, it tangles them up. It's hard...
15
16 **WARNER:** Amen.
17
18 **COMEY:** ... to share it within an investigative team. It's —
19 you have to be very careful about how you handle it, for
20 good reason.
21
22 So my thinking was, if I write it in such a way that I don't
23 include anything that would trigger a classification, that'll
24 make it easier for us to discuss, within the FBI and the
25 government, and to — to hold on to it in a way that makes
26 it accessible to us.
27
28 **WARNER:** Well, again, it's our hope, particularly since
29 you're a pretty knowledgeable guy and you wrote this in a
30 way that was unclassified, that this committee will get
31 access to that unclassified document. I think it'll be very
32 important to our investigation.
33

1 Let me just ask this in closing: How many ongoing
2 investigations, at any time, does the FBI have going on?
3
4 **(CROSSTALK)**
5
6 **COMEY:** Tens of thousands.
7
8 **WARNER:** Tens of thousands. Did the president ever ask
9 about any other ongoing investigation?
10
11 **COMEY:** No.
12
13 **WARNER:** Did he ever ask about you trying to interfere on
14 any other investigation?
15
16 **COMEY:** No.
17
18 **WARNER:** I think, again, this speaks volumes. This doesn't
19 even get to the questions around the — the phone calls
20 about lifting the cloud. I know other members will get to
21 that, but I really appreciate your testimony and appreciate
22 your service to our nation.
23
24 **COMEY:** Thank you, Senator Warner.
25
26 You know, I just — I'm sitting here, going through my
27 contacts with him. I had one conversation with the
28 president that was classified, where he asked about our —
29 an ongoing intelligence investigation. It was brief and
30 entirely professional.
31
32 **WARNER:** But he didn't ask you to take any specific action
33 on that...
34

1 **COMEY:** No, no.
2
3 **WARNER:** ... unlike what he had done vis-a-vis Mr. Flynn
4 and the overall Russia investigation?
5
6 **COMEY:** Correct.
7
8 **WARNER:** Thank you, sir.
9
10 **BURR:** Senator Risch?
11
12 **RISCH:** Thank you very much.
13
14 Mr. Comey, thank you for your service. America needs
15 more like you, and we really appreciate it.
16
17 **RISCH:** Yesterday, I got, and everybody got, the seven
18 pages of your direct testimony that's now a part of the
19 record, here. And the first — I read it, then I read it again,
20 and all I could think was, number one, how much I hated
21 the class of legal writing when I was in law school.
22
23 And you were the guy that probably got the A, after —
24 after reading this. So I — I find it clear, I find it concise and,
25 having been a prosecutor for a number of years and
26 handling hundred — maybe thousands of cases and read
27 police reports, investigative reports, this is as good as it
28 gets.
29
30 And — and I really appreciate that — not only — not only
31 the conciseness and the clearness of it, but also the fact
32 that you have things that were written down
33 contemporaneously when they happened, and you
34 actually put them in quotes, so we know exactly what

1 happened and we're — and we're not getting some
2 rendition of it that — that's in your mind. So...
3
4 **COMEY:** Thank you, Senator.
5
6 **RISCH:** ... so you're — you're to be complimented for that.
7
8 **COMEY:** I had great parents and great teachers who beat
9 that into me.
10
11 **(CROSSTALK)**
12
13 **RISCH:** That's obvious, sir.
14
15 The — the chairman walked you through a number of
16 things that — that the American people need to know and
17 want to know. Number one, obviously we're — all know
18 about the active measures that the Russians have taken.
19
20 I think a lot of people were surprised at this. Those of us
21 that work in the intelligence community didn't — it didn't
22 come as a surprise. But now, the American people know
23 this, and it's good they know this, because this is serious
24 and it's a problem.
25
26 I — I think, secondly, I gather from all this that you're
27 willing to say now that, while you were director, the
28 president of the United States was not under
29 investigation. Is that a fair statement?
30
31 **COMEY:** That's correct.
32
33 **RISCH:** All right. So that's a fact that we can rely at this...
34

1 **COMEY:** Yes, sir.
2
3 **RISCH:** ... OK.
4
5 On — I remember, you — you talked with us shortly after
6 February 14th, when the New York Times wrote an article
7 that suggested that the Trump campaign was colluding
8 with the Russians. You remember reading that article
9 when it first came out?
10
11 **COMEY:** I do. It was about allegedly extensive electronic
12 surveillance...
13
14 **RISCH:** Correct.
15
16 **(CROSSTALK)**
17
18 **COMEY:** ... communications. Yes, sir.
19
20 **RISCH:** And — and that upset you to the point where you
21 actually went out and surveyed the intelligence
22 community to see whether — whether you were missing
23 something in that. Is that correct?
24
25 **COMEY:** That's correct. I want to be careful in open
26 setting. But...
27
28 **RISCH:** I — I'm — I'm not going to any further than that
29 with it.
30
31 **COMEY:** OK.
32
33 **RISCH:** So thank you.
34

In addition to that, after that, you sought out both Republican and Democrat senators to tell them that, hey, I don't know where this is coming from, but this is not the — this is not factual. Do you recall that?

COMEY: Yes.

RISCH: OK. So — so, again, so the American people can understand this, that report by the New York Times was not true. Is that a fair statement?

COMEY: In — in the main, it was not true. And, again, all of you know this, maybe the American people don't. The challenge — and I'm not picking on reporters about writing stories about classified information, is that people talking about it often don't really know what's going on.

And those of us who actually know what's going on are not talking about it. And we don't call the press to say, hey, you got that thing wrong about this sensitive topic. We just have to leave it there.

I mentioned to the chairman the nonsense around what influenced me to make the July 5th statement. Nonsense, but I can't go explaining how it's nonsense.

RISCH: Thank you.

All right. So — so those three things, we now know, regarding the active measures, whether (sic) the president's under investigation and the collusion between the — the Russian — the Trump campaign and the Russians.

1 I — I want to drill right down, as my time is limited, to the
2 most recent dust-up regarding allegations that the
3 president of the United States obstructed justice. And,
4 boy, you nailed this down on page 5, paragraph 3. You put
5 this in quotes — words matter.
6
7 You wrote down the words so we can all have the words in
8 front of us now. There's 28 words there that are in quotes,
9 and it says, quote, "I hope" — this is the president
10 speaking — "I hope you can see your way clear to letting
11 this go, to letting Flynn go. He is a good guy. I hope you
12 can let this go."
13
14 Now those are his exact words, is that correct?
15
16 **COMEY:** Correct.
17
18 **RISCH:** And you wrote them here, and you put them in
19 quotes?
20
21 **COMEY:** Correct.
22
23 **RISCH:** Thank you for that. He did not direct you to let it
24 go.
25
26 **COMEY:** Not in his words, no.
27
28 **RISCH:** He did not order you to let it go.
29
30 **COMEY:** Again, those words are not an order.
31
32 **RISCH:** He said, "I hope." Now, like me, you probably did
33 hundreds of cases, maybe thousands of cases charging
34 people with criminal offenses. And, of course, you have

1 knowledge of the thousands of cases out there that —
2 where people have been charged.
3
4 Do you know of any case where a person has been
5 charged for obstruction of justice or, for that matter, any
6 other criminal offense, where this — they said, or thought,
7 they hoped for an outcome?
8
9 **COMEY:** I don't know well enough to answer. And the
10 reason I keep saying his words is I took it as a direction.
11
12 **RISCH:** Right.
13
14 **COMEY:** I mean, this is the president of the United States,
15 with me alone, saying, "I hope" this. I took it as, this is
16 what he wants me to do.
17
18 **(CROSSTALK)**
19
20 **COMEY:** Now I — I didn't obey that, but that's the way I
21 took it.
22
23 **RISCH:** You — you may have taken it as a direction, but
24 that's not what he said.
25
26 **(CROSSTALK)**
27
28 **COMEY:** Correct. I — that's why...
29
30 **RISCH:** He said — he said, "I hope."
31
32 **COMEY:** Those are exact words, correct.
33

1 **RISCH:** OK, do you (sic) — you don't know of anyone that's
2 ever been charged for hoping something. Is that a fair
3 statement?
4
5 **COMEY:** I don't, as I sit here.
6
7 **RISCH:** Yeah. Thank you.
8
9 Thank you, Mr. Chairman.
10
11 **BURR:** Senator Feinstein?
12
13 **FEINSTEIN:** Thanks very much, Mr. Chairman.
14
15 Mr. Comey, I just want you to know that I have great
16 respect for you. Senator Cornyn and I sit on the Judiciary
17 Committee, so we have occasion to have you before us.
18 And I know that you're a man of strength and integrity,
19 and I really regret the situation that we all find ourselves
20 in. I just want to say that.
21
22 Let me begin with one overarching question. Why do you
23 believe you were fired?
24
25 **COMEY:** Guess I don't know for sure. I believe the — I take
26 the president at his word, that I was fired because of the
27 Russia investigation. Something about the way I was
28 conducting it, the president felt, created pressure on him
29 that he wanted to relieve.
30
31 Again, I didn't know that at the time, but I watched his
32 interview, I've read the press accounts of his
33 conversations. So I take him at his word there.
34

Now, look, I — I could be wrong. Maybe he's saying something that's not true. But I take him at his word, at least based on what I know now.

FEINSTEIN: Talk for a moment about his request that you pledge loyalty, and your response to that and what impact you believe that had.

COMEY: I — I don't know for sure, because I don't know the president well enough to read him well. I think it was — because our relationship didn't get off to a great start, given the conversation I had to have on January 6th, this was not — this didn't improve the relationship, because it was very, very awkward.

He was asking for something, and I was refusing to give it. But again, I don't know him well enough to know how he reacted to that, exactly.

FEINSTEIN: Do you believe the Russia investigation played a role?

COMEY: In why I was fired?

FEINSTEIN: Yes.

COMEY: Yes, because I've seen the president say so.

FEINSTEIN: OK. Let's — let's go to the Flynn issue.

Senator Risch outlined a — "I hope you could see your way (sic) to letting Flynn go. He's a good guy. I hope you can let this go."

But you also said, in your written remarks, and I quote, that you had "understood the president to be requesting that we drop any investigation of Flynn in connection with false statements about his conversations with the Russian ambassador in December," end quote.

FEINSTEIN: Please go into that with more detail.

COMEY: Well, the — the context and the president's words are what led me to that conclusion.

As I said in my statement, I could be wrong, but Flynn had been forced to resign the day before, and — and the controversy around General Flynn at that point in time was centered on whether he had lied to the vice president about the nature of his conversations with the Russians, whether he had been candid with others in the course of that.

And so that happens on the day before. On the 14th, the president makes specific reference to that. And so that's why I understood him to be saying that what he wanted me to do was drop any investigation connected to Flynn's account of his conversations with the Russians.

FEINSTEIN: Now, here's the question: You're big. You're strong. I know the Oval Office, and I know what happens to people when they walk in. There is a certain amount of intimidation. But why didn't you stop and say, "Mr. President, this is wrong. I cannot discuss this with you"?

COMEY: It's a great question. Maybe if I were stronger, I would have. I was so stunned by the conversation that I just...

1
2 **(CROSSTALK)**
3
4 **COMEY:** ... took it in. And the only thing I could think to
5 say, because I was playing in my mind, because I could (sic)
6 remember every word he said — I was playing in my mind,
7 what should my response be? And that's why I very
8 carefully chose the words.
9
10 And, look, I — I've seen the tweet about tapes. Lordy, I
11 hope there are tapes. I — I remember saying, "I agree he's
12 a good guy," as a way of saying, "I'm not agreeing with
13 what you just asked me to do."
14
15 Again, maybe other people would be stronger in that
16 circumstance but that — that was — that's how I
17 conducted myself. I — I hope I'll never have another
18 opportunity. Maybe if I did it again, I would do it better.
19
20 **FEINSTEIN:** You described two phone calls that you
21 received from President Trump, one on March 30 and one
22 on April 11, where he, quote, "described the Russia
23 investigation as a cloud that was impairing his ability," end
24 quote, as president, and asked you, quote, "to lift the
25 cloud," end quote.
26
27 What — how did you interpret that? And what did you
28 believe he wanted you to do?
29
30 **COMEY:** I interpreted that as he was frustrated that the
31 Russia investigation was taking up so much time and
32 energy, I — I think he meant, of the executive branch, but
33 in the — in the public square in general, and it was making

it difficult for him to focus on other priorities of his. But
what he asked me was actually narrower than that.

COMEY: So I think what he meant by the cloud, and again,
I could be wrong, but what I think he meant by the cloud
was the entire investigation is — is taking up oxygen and
making it hard for me to focus on the things I want to
focus on.

The ask was to get it out that I, the president, am not
personally under investigation.

FEINSTEIN: After April 11th, did he ask you more, ever,
about the Russia investigation? Did he ask you any
questions?

COMEY: We never spoke again after April 11th.

FEINSTEIN: You told the president, I — I would see what
we could do. What did you mean?

COMEY: Well, it (sic) was kind of a slightly cowardly way of
trying to avoid telling him, we're not going to do that —
that I would see what we could do. It was a way of kind of
getting off the phone, frankly. And then I turned and
handed it to the acting deputy attorney general, Mr.
Boente.

FEINSTEIN: So I wanted to go into that. Who did you talk
with about that — lifting the cloud, stopping the
investigation — back at the FBI, and what was their
response?

COMEY: Well, the FBI, during one of the two conversations — I'm not remembering exactly. I think the first — my chief of staff was actually sitting in front of me, and heard my end of the conversation, because the president's call was a surprise.

And I discussed the lifting the cloud and the request with the senior leadership team, who in — in — typically, and I think in all these circumstances, was the deputy director, my chief of staff, the general counsel, the deputy director's chief counsel and, I think, in a number of circumstances, the number three in the FBI, and a few of the conversations included the head of the national security branch, so that group of us that lead the FBI when it comes to national security.

FEINSTEIN: OK. You have the president of the United States asking you to stop an investigation that's an important investigation. What was the response of your colleagues?

COMEY: I think they were as shocked and troubled by it as I was. Some said things that led me to believe that. I don't remember exactly, but the reaction was similar to mine. They're all experienced people who had never experienced such a thing. So they were very concerned.

And then the conversation turned to about, so what should we do with this information? And that was a struggle for us, because we are the leaders of the FBI. So it's been reported to us, in that I heard it and now I've shared it with the leaders of the FBI — our — our conversation was, should we share this with any senior officials at the Justice Department?

Our — our absolute primary concern was, we can't infect the investigative team. We don't want the agents and analysts working on this to know the president of the United States has — has asked — and when it comes from the president, I took it as a direction — to get rid of this investigation, because we're not going to follow that — that request.

And so we decided we gotta keep it away from our troops. But is there anybody else we ought to tell at the Justice Department? And, as I laid out in my — in my statement, we considered whether to tell the attorney general, decided that didn't make sense because we believed, rightly, that he was shortly going to recuse.

There were no other Senate-confirmed leaders in the Justice Department at that point. The deputy attorney general was Mr. Boente, who was acting and going to be shortly in that seat. And we decided the best move would be to hold it, keep it in a box, document it as we'd already done, and then this investigation's going to go on — figure out what to do with it down the road.

Is there way to corroborate this? Our view, at the time, was, look, it's your word against the president's. There's no way to corroborate this. That — my view of that changed when the prospect of tapes was raised, but that's how we thought about it then.

FEINSTEIN: Thank you. Thank you, Mr. Chairman.

BURR: Senator Rubio.

1 **RUBIO:** Thank you.
2
3 Director Comey, the meeting in the Oval Office where he
4 made the request about Mike Flynn — was that the only
5 time he asked you to hopefully let it go?
6
7 **COMEY:** Yes.
8
9 **RUBIO:** And in that meeting, as you understood it, that
10 was — he was asking not about the general Russia
11 investigation, he was asking very specifically about the
12 jeopardy that Flynn was in himself?
13
14 **COMEY:** That's how I understood it, yes, sir.
15
16 **RUBIO:** And as you perceived it, while it was a request that
17 — he hoped you did away with it, you perceived it as an
18 order, given his position, the setting and the like, and
19 some of the circumstances?
20
21 **COMEY:** Yes.
22
23 **RUBIO:** At the time, did you say anything to the president
24 about — that is not an appropriate request, or did you tell
25 the White House counsel, that is not an appropriate
26 request, someone needs to go tell the president that he
27 can't do these things?
28
29 **COMEY:** I didn't, no.
30
31 **RUBIO:** OK. Why?
32

COMEY: I don't know. I think the — as I said earlier, I think the circumstances were such that it was — I was a bit stunned, and didn't have the presence of mind.

And I don't know — you know, I don't want to make you — sound like I'm Captain Courageous. I don't know whether, even if I had the presence of mind, I would have said to the president, "Sir, that's wrong." I don't know whether I would have.

RUBIO: OK.

COMEY: But in the moment, it — it didn't — it didn't come to my mind. What came to my mind is, be careful what you say. And so I said, "I agree Flynn is a good guy."

RUBIO: So, on the cloud — we keep talking about this cloud — you perceived the cloud to be the Russian investigation in general, correct?

COMEY: Yes, sir.

RUBIO: But the specific ask was that you would tell the American people what you had already told him, what you had already told the leaders of Congress, both Democrats and Republicans: that he was not personally under investigation.

COMEY: Yes, sir, that's how I...

RUBIO: In fact (sic), he was asking you to do what you have done here today.

COMEY: ... correct. Yes, sir.

1
2 **RUBIO:** OK. And again, at that setting, did you say to the
3 president that it would be inappropriate for you to do so,
4 and then talk to the White House counsel or anybody so
5 hopefully they would talk to him and tell him that he
6 couldn't do this?
7
8 **COMEY:** First time, I said, "I'll see what we can do." Second
9 time, I explained how it should work, that the White House
10 counsel should contact the deputy attorney general.
11
12 **RUBIO:** You told him that?
13
14 **COMEY:** The president said, OK, then I think that's what I'll
15 do.
16
17 **RUBIO:** And just to be clear, for you to make a public
18 statement that he was not under investigation would not
19 have been illegal, but you felt it made no sense because it
20 could potentially create a duty to correct, if circumstances
21 changed?
22
23 **COMEY:** Yes, sir. We wrestled with it before my testimony
24 where I confirmed that there was an investigation. And
25 there were two primary concerns. One was it creates a
26 duty to correct, which I've lived before, and you want to
27 be very careful about doing that.
28
29 And second, it's a slippery slope, because if we say the
30 president and the vice president aren't under
31 investigation, what's the principled basis for — for
32 stopping?
33
34 **RUBIO:** OK.

1
2 **COMEY:** And so the leadership at — at justice, Acting
3 Attorney General Boente, said, "You're not going to do
4 that."
5
6 **RUBIO:** Now, on March 30th, during the phone call about
7 General Flynn, you said he abruptly shifted and brought up
8 something that you call, quote, unquote, "the McCabe
9 thing." Specifically, the McCabe thing, as you understood
10 it, was that McCabe's wife had received campaign money
11 from what I assume means Terry McAuliffe...
12
13 **COMEY:** Yes, sir.
14
15 **(CROSSTALK)**
16
17 **RUBIO:** ... who (sic) was very close to the Clintons. And —
18 and so why did you — had the president at any point in
19 time expressed to you concern, opposition, potential
20 opposition to McCabe? "I don't like this guy because he
21 got money from someone this close to Clinton?"
22
23 **COMEY:** He had asked me, during previous conversations,
24 about Andy McCabe, and said, in essence, "How's he going
25 to be with me as president? I was pretty rough on them
26 (sic) on the campaign trail." And...
27
28 **RUBIO:** He was rough on McCabe?
29
30 **COMEY:** ... he was — by his own account, he said he was
31 rough on McCabe and Mrs. McCabe on the campaign trail
32 — how's he going to be? And I assured the president, Andy
33 is a total pro. No issue at all. You got to know the people of
34 the FBI, they are not...

1
2 **(CROSSTALK)**
3
4 **RUBIO:** So — so, when the president turns to you and
5 says, "Remember, I never brought up the McCabe thing
6 because you said he was a good guy," did you perceive
7 that to be a statement that — I took care of you, I — I
8 didn't do something because you told me he was a good
9 guy. So now, you know, I'm asking you, potentially, for
10 something in return? Is that how you perceived it?
11
12 **COMEY:** I wasn't sure what to make of it, honestly. That's
13 possible, but it — it was so out of context that I didn't have
14 a clear view of what it was.
15
16 **RUBIO:** Now, on a number of occasions here, you bring up
17 — let's talk (sic) now about the general Russia
18 investigation, OK? In page 6 of your testimony, you say —
19 the first thing you say is, he asked what we could do to,
20 quote/unquote, "lift the cloud," the general Russia
21 investigation.
22
23 And you responded that we were investigating the matter
24 as quickly as we could and that there would be great
25 benefit, if we didn't find anything, to having done the work
26 well. And he agreed. He reemphasized the problems it was
27 causing him, but he agreed.
28
29 So, in essence, the president agreed with your statement
30 that it would be great if we could have an investigation, all
31 the facts came out and we found nothing. So he agreed
32 that that would be ideal, but this cloud is still messing up
33 my ability to do the rest of my agenda. Is that an accurate
34 assessment of...

1
2 **(CROSSTALK)**
3
4 <u>**COMEY:**</u> Yes, sir. He actually went farther than that. He —
5 he said, "And if some of my satellites did something
6 wrong, it'd be good to find that out."
7
8 <u>**RUBIO:**</u> Well, that's the second part, and that is the
9 satellites. He said, "If (sic) one of my satellites" — I
10 imagine, by that, he meant some of the other people
11 surrounding his campaign — "did something wrong, it
12 would be great to know that, as well"?
13
14 <u>**COMEY:**</u> Yes, sir. That's what he said.
15
16 <u>**RUBIO:**</u> So are those the other — are those the only two
17 instances in which that sort of back-and-forth happened,
18 where the president was basically saying, and I'm
19 paraphrasing here, it's OK, do the Russia investigation. I
20 hope it all comes out. I have nothing to do with anything
21 Russia. It'd be great if it all came out, if people around me
22 were doing things that were wrong.
23
24 <u>**COMEY:**</u> Yes. As I — I recorded it accurately there. That
25 was the sentiment he was expressing. Yes, sir.
26
27 <u>**RUBIO:**</u> So what it basically (sic) comes down to is the
28 president has asked three things of you. He asked for your
29 loyalty, and you said you would be loyally honest.
30
31 <u>**COMEY:**</u> Honestly loyal.
32
33 <u>**RUBIO:**</u> Honestly loyal. The — the — he asked you, on one
34 occasion, to let the Mike Flynn thing go because he was a

1 good guy — but (sic) you're aware that he said the exact
2 same thing in the press the next day. "He's a good guy,"
3 "He's been treated unfairly," et cetera, et cetera. So I
4 imagine your FBI agents read that.
5
6 **(CROSSTALK)**
7
8 **COMEY:** I'm sure they did.
9
10 **RUBIO:** Your — the president's wishes were known to
11 them, certainly, by the next day, when he had a press
12 conference with the prime minister.
13
14 **RUBIO:** But going back, the three requests were; number
15 one, be loyal; number two, let the Mike Flynn thing go,
16 he's a good guy, he's been treated unfairly; and, number
17 three, can you please tell the American people what these
18 leaders in Congress already know, what you already know,
19 what you've told me three times — that I'm not under —
20 personally under investigation?
21
22 **COMEY:** Those are the three things he asked. Yes, sir.
23
24 **RUBIO:** You know, this investigation is full of leaks, left and
25 right. I mean, we've learned more from the newspapers
26 sometimes than we do from our open hearings, for sure.
27
28 You ever wonder why, of all the things in this investigation,
29 the only thing that's never been leaked is the fact that the
30 president was not personally under investigation, despite
31 the fact that both Democrats and Republicans in (sic) the
32 leadership of Congress knew that, and have known that
33 for weeks?
34

1 **COMEY:** I don't know. I find matters that are briefed to the
2 Gang of Eight are pretty tightly held, in my experience.
3
4 **RUBIO:** Finally, who are those senior leaders at the FBI
5 that you shared these conversations with?
6
7 **COMEY:** As I said in response to Senator Feinstein's
8 question, deputy director, my chief of staff, general
9 counsel, the deputy director's chief counsel, and then,
10 more often than not, the number three person at the FBI,
11 who is the associate deputy director, and then, quite
12 often, the head of the national security branch.
13
14 **BURR:** Senator Wyden.
15
16 **WYDEN:** Thank you, Mr. Chairman.
17
18 Mr. Comey, welcome. You and I have had significant policy
19 differences over the years, particularly protecting
20 Americans' access to secure encryption. But I believe the
21 timing of your firing stinks.
22
23 And yesterday, you put on the record testimony that
24 demonstrates why the odor of presidential abuse of power
25 is so strong.
26
27 Now, to my questions. In talking to Senator Warner about
28 this dinner that you had with president, I believe, January
29 27th, all in one dinner, the president raised your job
30 prospects, he asked for your loyalty and denied allegations
31 against him — all took place over one supper.
32
33 **WYDEN:** Now, you told Senator Warner that the president
34 was looking to, quote, "get something." Looking back, did

1 that dinner suggest that your job might be contingent on
2 how you handled the investigation?
3
4 **COMEY:** I don't know that I'd go that far. I — I got the
5 sense my job would be contingent upon how he felt I —
6 excuse me — how he felt I conducted myself and whether
7 I demonstrated loyalty. But I don't know whether I'd go so
8 far as to connect it to the investigation (sic).
9
10 **(CROSSTALK)**
11
12 **WYDEN:** You said the president was trying to create some
13 sort of patronage relationship. In a patronage relationship
14 isn't the underling expected to behave in a manner
15 consistent with the wishes of the boss?
16
17 **COMEY:** Yes.
18
19 **WYDEN:** OK.
20
21 **COMEY:** Or at least consider how what you're doing will
22 affect the boss as a significant consideration.
23
24 **WYDEN:** Let me turn to the Attorney General. In your
25 statement, you said that you and the FBI leadership team
26 decided not to discuss the president's actions with
27 Attorney General Sessions, even though he had not
28 recused himself.
29
30 What was it about the Attorney General's own interactions
31 with the Russians, or his behavior with regard to the
32 investigation, that would have led the entire leadership of
33 the FBI to make this decision?
34

1 **COMEY:** Our judgment, as I recall, was that he was very
2 close to and inevitably going to recuse himself for a variety
3 of reasons. We also were aware of facts that I can't discuss
4 in an open setting that would make his continued
5 engagement in a Russia-related investigation problematic.
6
7 And so we were — we were convinced — and, in fact, I
8 think we had already heard that the career people were
9 recommending that he recuse himself — that he was not
10 going to be in contact with Russia- related matters much
11 longer, and that turned out to be the case.
12
13 **WYDEN:** How would you characterize Attorney General
14 Sessions's adherence to his recusal, in particular with
15 regard to his involvement in your firing, which the
16 president has acknowledged was because of the Russian
17 investigation?
18
19 **COMEY:** That's a question I can't answer. I think it's a
20 reasonable question. If — if, as the president said, I was
21 fired because of the Russia investigation, why was the
22 attorney general involved in that chain? I don't know, and
23 so I don't have an answer for the question.
24
25 **WYDEN:** Your testimony was that the president's request
26 about Flynn could infect the investigation. Had the
27 president got what he wanted and what he asked of you,
28 what would have been the effect on the investigation?
29
30 **COMEY:** Well we would have closed any investigation of
31 General Flynn in connection with his statements and
32 encounter — statements about and encounters (sic) with
33 Russians in the late part of December.
34

1 **WYDEN:** Well...

2

3 **(CROSSTALK)**

4

5 **COMEY:** So we — we would have dropped an open
6 criminal investigation.

7

8 **WYDEN:** So, in effect, when you talk about infecting the
9 enterprise, you would have dropped something major that
10 would have spoken to the overall ability of the American
11 people to get the facts?

12

13 **COMEY:** Correct. And — and, as good as our people are,
14 our judgment was we don't want them hearing that the
15 president of the United States wants this to go away,
16 because it might have an effect of their ability to be fair
17 and impartial and aggressive.

18

19 **WYDEN:** Now, the — Acting Attorney General Yates found
20 out that Michael Flynn could be blackmailed by the
21 Russians, and she went immediately to warn the White
22 House.

23

24 Flynn is gone, but other individuals with contacts with the
25 Russians are still in extremely important positions of
26 power. Should the American people have the same sense
27 of urgency now, with respect to them?

28

29 **COMEY:** I think all I can say, Senator, is it's a — the special
30 counsel's investigation is very important. Understanding
31 what efforts there were or are by the Russian government
32 to influence our government is a critical part of the FBI's
33 mission, so — and you've got the right person in Bob
34 Mueller to lead it.

1
2 So it's a very important piece of work.
3
4 **WYDEN:** Vice President Pence was the head of the
5 transition. To your knowledge, was he aware of the
6 concerns about Michael Flynn prior to or during General
7 Flynn's tenure as national security adviser?
8
9 **COMEY:** I don't — you're asking — including up to the
10 time when Flynn was...
11
12 **WYDEN:** Right (sic).
13
14 **COMEY:** ... forced to resign? My understanding is that he
15 was, and I'm trying to remember where I get that
16 understanding from — I think from Acting Attorney
17 General Yates.
18
19 **WYDEN:** So former Acting Attorney General Yates testified
20 that concerns about General Flynn were discussed with
21 the intelligence community. Would that have included
22 anyone at the CIA or Dan Coats' office at the DNI?
23
24 **COMEY:** I would assume yes.
25
26 **WYDEN:** Michael Flynn resigned four days after Attorney
27 General Sessions was sworn in. Do you know if the
28 attorney general was aware of the concerns about Michael
29 Flynn during that period?
30
31 **COMEY:** I don't, as I sit here — I don't — I don't recall that
32 he was. I could be wrong, but I don't remember that he
33 was.
34

1 **WYDEN:** And, finally, let's see if you can give us some
2 sense of who recommended your firing. Besides the letters
3 from the attorney general, the deputy attorney general,
4 do you have any information on who may have
5 recommended or have been involved in your firing?
6
7 **COMEY:** I don't. I don't.
8
9 **WYDEN:** OK (sic).
10
11 Thank you, Mr. Chairman.
12
13 **BURR:** Senator Collins.
14
15 **COLLINS:** Thank you, Mr. Chairman.
16
17 Mr. Comey, let me begin by thanking you for your
18 voluntary compliance with our request to appear before
19 this committee, and it's discussing (sic) this very important
20 investigation.
21
22 I want, first, to ask you about your conversations with the
23 president, the three conversations in which you told him
24 that he was not under investigation.
25
26 The first was during your January 6th meeting, according
27 to your testimony, in which it appears that you actually
28 volunteered that assurance. Is that correct?
29
30 **COMEY:** That's correct.
31
32 **COLLINS:** Did you limit that statement to
33 counterintelligence investigations, or were you talking
34 about any kind of FBI investigation?

1
2 **COMEY:** I didn't — I didn't use the term
3 "counterintelligence." I was speaking to him, and briefing
4 him about some salacious and unverified material. It was
5 in the context of that that he had a strong and defensive
6 reaction about that not being true. And my reading of it
7 was it was important for me to assure him we were not
8 personally investigating him. And so the context then was
9 actually narrower, focused on what I had just talked to him
10 about.
11
12 It was very important because it was, first, true. And
13 second, I was worried very much about being in kind of a
14 — kind of a J. Edgar Hoover-type situation. I didn't want
15 him thinking that I was briefing him on this to sort of hang
16 it over him in some way. I was briefing him on it because
17 we were (sic) — had been told by the media it was about
18 to launch. We didn't want to be keeping that from him.
19
20 **COMEY:** And if there was some — he needed to know this
21 was being said. But I was very keen not to leave him with
22 an impression that the bureau was trying to do something
23 to him. And so that's the context in which I said, "Sir, we're
24 not personally investigating you."
25
26 **COLLINS:** And then, on — and that's why you volunteered
27 the information...
28
29 **COMEY:** Yes, ma'am.
30
31 **COLLINS:** ... correct?
32
33 Then, on the January 27th dinner, you show — you told
34 the president that he should be careful about asking you

to investigate, because, quote, "You might create a narrative that we are investigating him personally," which we weren't.

Again, were you limiting that statement to counterintelligence investigations, or more broadly, such as a criminal investigation?

COMEY: The context was very similar. I didn't — I didn't modify the word "investigation." It was — again, he was reacting strongly again to that unverified material, saying, "I'm tempted to order you to investigate it." And that — in the context of that, I said "Sir, you want to be careful about that, because it might create a narrative we're investigating you personally."

COLLINS: And then there was the March 30th phone call in — with the president, in which you reminded him that congressional leaders have been briefed that we were not personally — the FBI was not personally investigating President Trump.

And again, was that statement to congressional leaders and to the president limited to counterintelligence investigations? Or was it a broader statement?

(CROSSTALK)

COLLINS: I'm trying to understand whether there was any kind of investigation of the president under way.

COMEY: No. I'm sorry, and — and if I misunderstood, I apologize. We briefed the congressional leadership about what Americans we had opened counterintelligence investigation cases on, and we specifically said the president is not one of those Americans, but — that there was no other investigation of the president that we were not mentioning at that time.

What (sic) — the context was counterintelligence, but I wasn't trying to hide some criminal investigation of the president.

COLLINS: And was the president under investigation at the time of your dismissal on May 9th?

COMEY: No.

COLLINS: I'd like to now turn to the conversations with the president about Michael Flynn, which have been discussed at great length. And, first, let me make very clear that the president never should have cleared the room, and he never should have asked you, as you reported, to let it go — to let the investigation go.

But I remain puzzled by your response. Your response was, "I agree that Michael Flynn is a good guy." You could have said, "Mr. President, this meeting is inappropriate. This response could compromise the investigation. You should not be making such a request."

It's fundamental to the operation of our government that the FBI be insulated from this kind of political pressure. And you've talked a bit today about that you were stunned by the president making the request.

But my question to you is, later on, upon reflection, did you go to anyone at the Department of Justice and ask

1   them to call the White House counsel's office and explain
2   that the president had to have a far better understanding
3   and appreciation of his role vis-a-vis the FBI?
4
5   **COMEY:** In general, I did. I spoke to the attorney general,
6   and I spoke to the new deputy attorney general, Mr.
7   Rosenstein, when he took office, and explained my serious
8   concern about the way in which the president is
9   interacting, especially with the FBI.
10
11 And I specifically, as I said my testimony, asked the — told
12 the attorney general, it can't happen that you get kicked
13 out of the room and the president talks to me.
14
15 Look, in the room — and — and — but why didn't we raise
16 the specific (sic)? It was of investigative interest us to try
17 and figure out, so — what just happened with the
18 president's request. So I would not have wanted to alert
19 the White House that it had happened until we figured
20 out, what are we going to do with this investigatively?
21
22 **COLLINS:** Your testimony was that you went to Attorney
23 General Sessions and said, "Don't ever leave me alone
24 with him again." Are you saying that you also told him that
25 he had made a request that you let it go, with regard to
26 part of the investigation of Michael Flynn?
27
28 **COMEY:** No, I specifically did not. I did not.
29
30 **COLLINS:** OK, you mentioned that, from your very first
31 meeting with the president, you decided to write a memo
32 memorializing the conversation. What was it about that
33 very first meeting that made you write a memo, when you
34 had not done that with two previous presidents?

1

2 **COMEY:** As I said, a combination of things. A gut feeling is
3 an important overlay on it (sic). But the circumstances —
4 that I was alone, the subject matter, and the nature of the
5 person that I was interacting with and my read of that
6 person.

7

8 (UNKNOWN): The nature of that person (sic)?

9

10 **COMEY:** Yeah, and — and — and, really, just a gut feel,
11 laying on top of all of that, that this — it's going to be
12 important, to protect this organization, that I make
13 records of this.

14

15 **COLLINS:** And finally, did you show copies of your memos
16 to anyone outside of the Department of Justice?

17

18 **COMEY:** Yes.

19

20 **COLLINS:** And to whom did you show copies?

21

22 **COMEY:** I asked — the president tweeted on Friday, after I
23 got fired, that I better hope there's not tapes. I woke up in
24 the middle of the night on Monday night, because it didn't
25 dawn on me originally that there might be corroboration
26 for our conversation. There might be a tape.

27

28 And my judgment was, I needed to get that out into the
29 public square. And so I asked a friend of mine to share the
30 content of the memo with a reporter. Didn't do it myself,
31 for a variety of reasons. But I asked him to, because I
32 thought that might prompt the appointment of a special
33 counsel. And so I asked a close friend of mine to do it.

34

1 **COLLINS:** And was that Mr. Wittes?
2
3 **COMEY:** No, no.
4
5 **COLLINS:** Who was that?
6
7 **COMEY:** A good friend of mine who's a professor at
8 Columbia Law School.
9
10 **COLLINS:** Thank you.
11
12 **BURR:** Senator Heinrich?
13
14 **HEINRICH:** Mr. Comey, prior to January 27th of this year,
15 have you ever had a one-on-one meeting or — or a private
16 dinner with a president of the United States?
17
18 **COMEY:** No, I met — dinner, no. I had two one-on-ones
19 with President Obama that I laid out in my testimony:
20 once, to talk about law enforcement issues — law
21 enforcement and race, which was an important topic
22 throughout for me and for the president; and then once,
23 very briefly, for him to say goodbye.
24
25 **HEINRICH:** Were those brief interactions?
26
27 **COMEY:** No. The one about law enforcement and race in
28 policing, we spoke for probably over an hour, just the two
29 of us.
30
31 **HEINRICH:** How unusual is it to have a — a one-on-one
32 dinner with the president? Did that strike you as odd?
33

1 **COMEY:** Yeah, so much so that I assumed there would be
2 others — that he couldn't possibly be having dinner with
3 me alone.
4
5 **HEINRICH:** If — do you have an impression that, if you had
6 found — if you had behaved differently in that dinner —
7 and I am quite pleased that you did not — but if you had
8 found a way to express some sort of expression of loyalty,
9 or given some suggestion that the Flynn criminal
10 investigation might be pursued less vigorously, do you
11 think you would've still been fired?
12
13 **COMEY:** I don't know. I — it's impossible to say, looking
14 back. I don't know.
15
16 **HEINRICH:** But you felt like those two things were — were
17 directly relevant to your — the kind of relationship that
18 the president was seeking to establish with you?
19
20 **COMEY:** Sure, yes.
21
22 **HEINRICH:** The — the president has repeatedly talked
23 about the Russian investigation into the U.S. — or the
24 Russian — Russia's involvement in the U.S. election cycle
25 as a hoax and as fake news.
26
27 Can you talk a little bit about what you saw as FBI director
28 — and, obviously, only the parts that you can share in this
29 setting — that — that demonstrate how serious this action
30 actually was, and why there was an investigation in the
31 first place?
32
33 **COMEY:** Yes, sir.
34

The — there should be no fuzz on this whatsoever. The Russians interfered in our election during the 2016 cycle. They did it with purpose. They did it with sophistication. They did it with overwhelming technical efforts. And it was an active-measures campaign driven from the top of that government. There is no fuzz on that.

It is a high-confidence judgment of the entire intelligence community, and — and the members of this committee have — have seen the intelligence. It's not a close call. That happened. That's about as un-fake as you can possibly get, and is very, very serious, which is why it's so refreshing to see a bipartisan focus on that, because this is about America, not about any particular party.

HEINRICH: So that was a hostile act by the Russian government against this country?

COMEY: Yes, sir.

HEINRICH: Did the president, in any of those interactions that you've shared with us today, ask you what you should be doing, or what our government should be doing, or the intelligence community, to protect America against Russian interference in our election system?

COMEY: I don't recall a conversation like that.

HEINRICH: Never?

COMEY: No.

HEINRICH: Do you — do you find it odd...

1 (CROSSTALK)

2

3 **COMEY:** Not with — not with — not with President Trump.

4

5 **HEINRICH:** Right.

6

7 **COMEY:** I attended a fair number of meetings on that with
8 President Obama.

9

10 **HEINRICH:** Do you find it odd that the president seemed
11 unconcerned by Russia's actions in our election?

12

13 **COMEY:** I — I can't answer that, because I don't know
14 what other conversations he had with other advisers or
15 other intelligence community leaders. So I — I — I just
16 don't know, sitting here.

17

18 **HEINRICH:** Did you have any interactions with the
19 president that suggested he was taking that hostile action
20 seriously?

21

22 **COMEY:** I don't remember any interactions with the
23 president, other than the initial briefing on January the
24 6th. I don't remember — could be wrong, but I don't
25 remember any conversations with him at all about that.

26

27 **HEINRICH:** As you're very aware, it was only the two of
28 you in the room for that dinner. You've told us the
29 president asked you to back off the Flynn investigation.
30 The president told a reporter...

31

32 **COMEY:** Not in that dinner.

33

HEINRICH: Fair enough — told the (sic) reporter he did — never did that. You've testified that the president asked for your loyalty in that dinner. The White House denies that. A lot of this comes down to, who should we believe? Do you want to say anything as to why we should believe you?

COMEY: Probably (sic) — my mother raised me not to say things like this about myself, so not I'm going to. I think people should look at the whole body of my testimony, because, as I used to say to juries, and when I talked about a witness, you can't cherry-pick it. You can't say, "I like these things he said, but on this, he's a — he's a dirty, rotten liar."

HEINRICH: Right.

COMEY: You got to take it all together. And I've tried to be open and fair and transparent and accurate. A really significant fact to me is, so why did he kick everybody out of the Oval Office?

Why would you kick the attorney general, the president (sic), the chief of staff out, to talk to me, if it was about something else? And so that — that, to me, is — as an investigator, is a very significant fact.

HEINRICH: And as we look at — at testimony, or as — communication from both of you, we should probably be looking for consistency.

COMEY: Well, in looking at any witness, you look at consistency, track record, demeanor, record over time, that sort of thing.

1
2 **HEINRICH:** Thank you.
3
4 So there are reports that the incoming Trump
5 administration, either during the transition and/or after
6 the inauguration, attempted to set up a sort of back-door
7 communication channel with the Russian government
8 using their infrastructure, their devices or facilities.
9
10 What would be the risks particularly for a transition,
11 someone not actually in the office of the president yet, to
12 setting up unauthorized channels with a hostile foreign
13 government, especially if they were to evade our own
14 American intelligence services?
15
16 **COMEY:** I'm not going to comment on whether that
17 happened in an open setting. But the risk is — primary risk
18 is obvious: you spare the Russians the cost and effort of
19 having to break into our communications channels by
20 using theirs.
21
22 And so you make it a whole lot easier for them to capture
23 all of your conversations, and then to use those to the
24 benefit of Russia against the United States.
25
26 **HEINRICH:** The memos that you wrote — you wrote, did
27 you write all nine of them in a way that was designed to
28 prevent them from needing classification?
29
30 **COMEY:** No. And — and, on a few of the occasions, I wrote
31 — I sent e-mails to my chief of staff or others on some of
32 the brief phone conversations that I recall. The first one
33 was a classified briefing.
34

1 Although it wasn't in a SCIF, it was in a conference room at
2 Trump Tower. It was a classified briefing and so I wrote
3 that on a classified device. The one I started typing...
4
5 **HEINRICH:** Got you.
6
7 **COMEY:** ... in the car — that was a classified laptop that I
8 started working on.
9
10 **HEINRICH:** Any reason, in a classified environment, in a
11 SCIF, that this committee would — it would not be
12 appropriate to see those communications, from — at least
13 from your perspective as the author?
14
15 **COMEY:** No.
16
17 **HEINRICH:** Thank you, Mr. Chairman.
18
19 **BURR:** Senator Blunt.
20
21 **BLUNT:** Thank you, Mr. Chairman.
22
23 Mr. Comey, when you were terminated at the FBI, I said,
24 and still continue to feel, that you have provided years of
25 great service to the country.
26
27 I also said that I'd had significant questions, over the last
28 year, about some of the decision you made. If — if the
29 president hadn't terminated your service, would you still
30 be, in your opinion, the director of the FBI today?
31
32 **COMEY:** Yes, sir.
33

BLUNT: So you took as a direction from the president something that you thought was serious and troublesome, but continued to show up for work the next day?

COMEY: Yes, sir.

BLUNT: And, six weeks later we're still telling the — we're telling the president, on March the 30th, that he was not personally the target of any investigation?

COMEY: Correct. On March the 30th, and I think again on — I think on April 11th as well, I told him we're not investigating him personally. That was true.

BLUNT: Well, the point to me — the concern to me there is that all these things are going on. You, now, in retrospect — or at you, now, to this committee — that these were — you had serious concerns about what the president had, you believed, directed you to do, and had taken no action — hadn't even reported up the chain of command, assuming you believe there is an "up the chain of command," that these things had happened.

Do you have a sense of that, looking back, that that was a mistake?

COMEY: No. In fact, I think no action was the most important thing I could do to make sure there was no interference with the investigation.

BLUNT: And on the — on the Flynn issue specifically, I believe you said earlier that you believed the president was suggesting you drop any investigation of Flynn's account of his conversation with the Russian ambassador,

1   which was essentially misleading the vice president and
2   others?
3
4   **COMEY:** Correct, and — and I'm not going to go into the
5   details, but whether there were false statements made to
6   government investigators, as well.
7
8   **BLUNT:** The — any suggestion that the — that General
9   Flynn had violated the Logan Act, I always find pretty
10 incredible. The Logan Act's been on the books for over 200
11 years. Nobody's ever been prosecuted for violating the
12 Logan Act.
13
14 My sense would be that the discussion — not the problem
15 — misleading investigators or the vice president might
16 have been.
17
18 **COMEY:** That's fair. Yes, sir.
19
20 **BLUNT:** And — and you're — had you previously, on
21 February the 14th, discussed with the president, in the
22 previous meeting, anything your investigators had learned,
23 or their impressions from talking to Flynn?
24
25 **COMEY:** No, sir.
26
27 **BLUNT:** So he said, "He's a good guy." You said, "He's a
28 good guy." And that was — no further action taken on
29 that?
30
31 **COMEY:** Well, he said more than that. But there was no —
32 the action was I wrote it up, briefed our senior team, tried
33 to figure out what to do with it and just (sic) made a

1 decision, we're going to hold this and then see what we
2 make of it down the road.
3
4 **COMEY:** Yes, sir.
5
6 **BLUNT:** Was it your view that not briefing up (sic) meant
7 you really had no responsibility to report that to the
8 Justice Department in some way?
9
10 **COMEY:** I think, at some point — and — and I don't know
11 what Director Mueller is going to do with it, but at some
12 point I was sure we were going to brief it to the team in
13 charge of the case.
14
15 But our judgment was, in the short term, doesn't make
16 sense to — no fuzz on the fact that I reported it to the
17 attorney general. That's why I stressed he shouldn't be
18 kicked out of the room. But — didn't make sense to report
19 to him now.
20
21 **BLUNT:** You know, you said the attorney general said (sic),
22 "I don't want to be in the room with him alone again," but
23 you continued to talk to him on the phone. What is the
24 difference in being in the room alone with him and talking
25 to him on the phone alone?
26
27 **COMEY:** Yeah, I think that what I stressed (sic) to the
28 attorney general was a little broader than just the room. I
29 said "You — I report to you. It's very important you be
30 between me and the White House, between..."
31
32 **(CROSSTALK)**
33

1 **BLUNT:** After that discussion with the attorney general,
2 did you take phone calls from the president?
3
4 **COMEY:** Yes, sir.
5
6 **BLUNT:** So why did you just say you need to talk to — why
7 didn't you say, "I'm not taking that call. You need to talk to
8 the attorney general"?
9
10 **COMEY:** Well, I — I did, on the April 11th call, and I
11 reported the calls — the March 30th call and the April
12 11th call — to my superior, who was the acting deputy
13 attorney general.
14
15 **BLUNT:** I — I don't want to run out of time here. Let me
16 make one other point.
17
18 In reading your testimony, January the 3rd, January the
19 27th and March the 30th — it appears to me that, on all
20 three of those occasions, you, unsolicited by the president,
21 made the point to him that he was not a target of the — of
22 an investigation.
23
24 **COMEY:** Correct. Yes, sir.
25
26 **BLUNT:** One, I thought the March 30th very interesting.
27 You said, well, even though you don't want — you may not
28 want us — that was the 27th, where he said, "Why don't
29 you look into that dossier thing more?" You said, "Well,
30 you may not want that, because then we couldn't tell you
31 — couldn't say with — we couldn't answer the question
32 about you being a target of the investigation."
33

But you didn't seem to be answering that question anyhow. As Senator Rubio pointed out, the one unanswered, unleaked question seems to have been that, in this whole period of time.

But you said something earlier I don't want to fail to follow up on. You said, after you were dismissed, you gave information to a friend so that friend could get that information into the public media.

COMEY: Correct.

BLUNT: What kind of information was that? Wasn't that (sic) — what kind of information did you give to a friend?

COMEY: That the — the — the Flynn conversation, that the president asked me to let the — the Flynn — I'm forgetting my exact own words, but the — the conversation in the Oval Office.

BLUNT: So you didn't consider your memo or your sense of that conversation to be a government document? You consider it to be somehow your own personal document that you could share with the media as you wanted to?

COMEY: Correct. I...

BLUNT: Through a friend?

COMEY: ... I understood this to be my recollection, recorded, of my conversation with the president. As a private citizen, I felt free to share that. I thought it very important to get it out.

1 **BLUNT:** So were all of your memos that you've recorded
2 on classified or other documents memos that might be
3 yours as a private citizen?
4
5 **COMEY:** I'm sorry, I'm not following the question.
6
7 **BLUNT:** Well, I think you said you'd used classified — a
8 classified...
9
10 **(CROSSTALK)**
11
12 **COMEY:** Not the classified documents. Unclassified — I
13 don't have any of them anymore. I gave them to the
14 special counsel. But, yeah, my view was that the content
15 of those unclassified — the memorialization of those
16 conversations was my recollection recorded.
17
18 **BLUNT:** So why didn't you give those to somebody
19 yourself, rather than give them through a third party?
20
21 **COMEY:** Because I was worried the media was camping at
22 the end of my driveway at that point, and I was actually
23 going out of town with my wife to hide, and I worried it
24 would be like feeding seagulls at the beach...
25
26 **(LAUGHTER)**
27
28 ...if — if it was — if it was I who gave it to the media. So I
29 asked my friend, "Make sure this gets out."
30
31 **BLUNT:** It does seem to me that what you do there is
32 create a source close to the former director of the FBI, as
33 opposed to just taking responsibility yourself for saying,
34 "Here are these records."

1
2 And, like everybody else, I have other things I'd like to get
3 into, but I'm out of time.
4
5 **COMEY:** OK.
6
7 **BURR:** Senator King.
8
9 **KING:** Thank you.
10
11 First I'd like to acknowledge Senator Blumenthal and,
12 earlier, Senator Nelson. I think the one principal thing
13 you'll learn today, Senator, is that the chairs there are less
14 comfortable than the chairs here. But I welcome you to
15 the hearing.
16
17 Mr. Comey, a broad question. Was the Russian activity in
18 the 2016 election a one-off proposition? Or is this part of a
19 long-term strategy? Will they be back?
20
21 **COMEY:** Oh, it's a long-term practice of theirs. It — it
22 stepped up a notch in a significant way in '16. They'll be
23 back.
24
25 **KING:** I think that's very important for the American
26 people to understand, that this is — this is very much a
27 forward-looking investigation in terms of how do we
28 understand what they did and how do we prevent it.
29 Would you agree that that's a big part of our role here?
30
31 **COMEY:** Yes, sir, and it's not a Republican thing or
32 Democratic thing. It really is an American thing. They're
33 going to come for whatever party they choose to try and
34 work on behalf of. And they're — they're not devoted to

1 either, in my experience. They're just about their own
2 advantage. And they will be back.
3
4 **KING:** That's my observation. I don't think Putin is a
5 Republican or a Democrat. He's an opportunist.
6
7 **COMEY:** I think that's a fair statement.
8
9 **KING:** With regard to the — several of these
10 conversations, in his interview with Lester Holt on NBC,
11 the president said, "I had dinner with him. He wanted to
12 have dinner because he wanted to stay on." Is this an
13 accurate statement?
14
15 **COMEY:** No, sir.
16
17 **KING:** Did you, in any way, initiate that dinner?
18
19 **COMEY:** No, he — he called me at my desk at lunchtime,
20 and asked me was I free for dinner that night. I called
21 himself (sic) and said, "Can you come over for dinner
22 tonight?"
23
24 And I said, "Yes, sir."
25
26 He said, "Will 6 work?" I think he said 6 first. And then he
27 said, "I was going to invite your whole family, but we'll do
28 that next time. I wanted (sic) you to come over. And is — is
29 that a good time?"
30
31 I said, "Sir, whatever works for you."
32
33 And he then said, "How about 6:30?"
34

1 And I — I said, "Whatever works for you, sir." And then I
2 hung up and had to call my wife and break a date with her.
3 I was supposed to take her out to dinner that night, and
4 (OFF-MIKE).
5
6 **KING:** That's one of the all-time great excuses for breaking
7 a date.
8
9 **(LAUGHTER)**
10
11 **COMEY:** In retrospect, I would have — I love spending
12 time my wife. I wish I'd been there that night.
13
14 **(LAUGHTER)**
15
16 **KING:** That's one question I'm not going follow up, Mr.
17 Comey.
18
19 But, in that same interview, the president said, "In one
20 case, I called him, and in one case, he called me." Is that an
21 accurate statement?
22
23 **COMEY:** No.
24
25 **KING:** Did you ever call the president?
26
27 **COMEY:** No. I — I might — the only reason I'm hesitating is
28 I think there was a least one conversation where I was
29 asked to call the White House switchboard to be
30 connected to him, but I — I never initiated a
31 communication with the president.
32
33 **KING:** And, in his press conference on May 18th, the
34 president was asked whether he had urged you to shut

1 down the investigation into Michael Flynn. The president
2 responded, quote, "No, no. Next question." Is that an
3 accurate statement?
4
5 **COMEY:** I don't believe it is.
6
7 **KING:** Thank you.
8
9 With regard to the question of him being under personal
10 — personally under investigation, does that mean that the
11 dossier is not being reviewed or investigated or followed
12 up on in any way?
13
14 **COMEY:** I obviously can't — I can't comment either way. I
15 can't talk in an open setting about the investigation as it
16 was when I was the head of the FBI. And obviously it's —
17 it's Director Mueller's — Bob Mueller's responsibility now,
18 so I just — I don't know.
19
20 **KING:** So clearly your statements to the president back in
21 those — these various times when you assured him he
22 wasn't under investigation were as of that moment. That
23 — that correct, is it not?
24
25 **COMEY:** Correct — correct.
26
27 **KING:** Now, on the Flynn investigation, is it not true that
28 Mr. Flynn was and is a central figure in this entire
29 investigation of the relationship between the Trump
30 campaign and the Russians?
31
32 **COMEY:** I can't answer that in an open setting, sir.
33

1 **KING:** And certainly Mr. Flynn was part of the so-called
2 Russian investigation. Can you answer that question?
3
4 **COMEY:** I have to give you the same answer.
5
6 **KING:** All right. We'll be having a closed session shortly, so
7 we will follow up on that.
8
9 In terms of his comments to you about — I think in
10 response to Mr. Risch — to Senator Risch, you said he said,
11 "I hope you will hold back on that." But when you get a —
12 when a president of the United States in the Oval Office
13 says something like "I hope" or "I suggest" or — or "would
14 you," do you take that as a — as a — as a directive?
15
16 **COMEY:** Yes. Yes, it rings in my ear as kind of, "Will no one
17 rid me of this meddlesome priest?"
18
19 **KING:** I was just going to quote that. In 1170, December
20 29, Henry II said, "Who will rid me of this meddlesome
21 priest?" and then, the next day, he was killed — Thomas
22 Becket. That's exactly the same situation. You're — we're
23 thinking along the same lines.
24
25 Several other questions, and these are a little bit more
26 detailed. What do you know about the Russian bank, VEB?
27
28 **COMEY:** Nothing that I can talk about in an open setting. I
29 mean, I know it...
30
31 **(CROSSTALK)**
32
33 **KING:** Well, that takes care of my next three questions.
34

1 **COMEY:** I know it exists. Yes, sir.
2
3 **KING:** You know it exists. What is the relationship of
4 Ambassador — the ambassador from Russia to the United
5 States, to the Russian intelligence infrastructure?
6
7 **COMEY:** Well, he's a diplomat who is the chief of mission
8 at the Russian embassy, which employs a robust cohort of
9 intelligence officers. And so, surely, he's witting of their
10 very, very aggressive intelligence operations, at least some
11 of it in the United States. I don't — I don't consider him to
12 be an intelligence officer himself. He's a diplomat.
13
14 **KING:** Did you ever — did the FBI ever brief the Trump
15 administration about the — the advisability of interacting
16 directly with Ambassador Kislyak?
17
18 **COMEY:** Look (sic), all I can say sitting here is there were a
19 variety of defensive briefings given to the incoming
20 administration about the counterintelligence risk.
21
22 **KING:** Back to Mr. Flynn, would the — would closing out
23 the Flynn investigation have impeded the overall Russian
24 investigation?
25
26 **COMEY:** No. Well, unlikely, except to the extent — there's
27 always a possibility, if you have a criminal case against
28 someone and you bring in and squeeze them, you flip
29 them, and they give you information about something
30 else. But I saw the two as touching each other, but
31 separate.
32
33 **KING:** With regard to your memos, isn't it true that in a —
34 in a court case, when you're weighing evidence,

contemporaneous memos and contemporaneous statements to third parties are considered probative in terms of the — the — the validity of — of testimony?

COMEY: Yes.

KING: Thank you.

Thank you, Mr. Chairman.

BURR: Senator Cotton?

Or — excuse me, Senator Lankford?

LANKFORD: Well, Director Comey, good to see you again.

COMEY: You, too.

LANKFORD: We've had multiple opportunities to be able to visit, as everyone on this dais has. And I appreciate you and your service and what you have done for the nation for a long time, which you continue to do.

I've told you before in the heat (sic) of last year, when we had an opportunity to visit personally, that I pray for you and for your family, because you do carry a tremendous amount of stress. And that is still true today.

COMEY: Thank you.

LANKFORD: Let me — let me walk through a couple things with you. Your notes were obviously exceptionally important, because they give a very rapid account of what

1 you — what you wrote down and what you perceived to
2 happen in those different meetings.
3
4 Have you had the opportunity to be able to reference
5 those notes when you were preparing the written
6 statement that you put — for us today?
7
8 **COMEY:** Yes, I — yes. I think nearly all of my written
9 recordings of my conversations — had a chance to review
10 them before filing my statement.
11
12 **LANKFORD:** Do you have a copy of any those notes,
13 personally?
14
15 **COMEY:** I don't. I turned them over to Bob Mueller's
16 investigators.
17
18 **LANKFORD:** The individual that you told about your
19 memos, that then sent on to the New York Times — do
20 they have a copy of those memos, or were they told orally
21 of those memos?
22
23 **COMEY:** Had a copy — had a copy at the time.
24
25 **LANKFORD:** Do they — do they still have a copy of those
26 memos?
27
28 **COMEY:** That's a good question. I think so. I guess I can't
29 say for sure, sitting here, but I — I — I guess I don't know,
30 but I think so.
31
32 **LANKFORD:** So the question is, could you ask them to
33 hand that copy right back to you, so you could hand them
34 over to this committee?

1
2 **COMEY:** Potentially.
3
4 **LANKFORD:** I would like to move that from "potential" to
5 "see if we can ask that question," so we can have a copy of
6 those. Obviously those notes are exceptionally important
7 to us to be able to go through the process so we can — we
8 can continue to get to the facts as — as we see it. As you
9 know, the written documents are exceptionally important.
10
11 **LANKFORD:** Are there other documents that we need to
12 be aware of that you used in your preparation for your
13 written statement that we should also have, that would
14 assist us in helping with this?
15
16 **COMEY:** Not that I'm aware of, no.
17
18 **LANKFORD:** Past the February the 14th meeting which is a
19 very important meeting obviously, as we discuss the
20 conversations here about Michael Flynn. When the
21 president asked you about he hopes that you would let
22 this go, and the conversation back and forth about him
23 being a good guy.
24
25 After that time did the president ever bring up anything
26 about Michael Flynn again to you? You had multiple other
27 conversations you have (inaudible) with the president.
28
29 **COMEY:** No, I don't remember him ever bringing it up
30 again.
31
32 **LANKFORD:** Did any member of the White House staff
33 ever come to you and talk to you about letting go of the

1   Michael Flynn case, or dropping it or anything referring to
2   that?
3
4   **COMEY:** No, nope.
5
6   **LANKFORD:** Did the director of national intelligence come
7   to you and talk to you about that?
8
9   **COMEY:** No.
10
11   **LANKFORD:** Did anyone from the Attorney General's
12   office, the Department of Justice ask you about that?
13
14   **COMEY:** No.
15
16   **LANKFORD:** Did the head of NSA talk to you about that?
17
18   **COMEY:** No.
19
20   **LANKFORD:** The — the key aspect here is, if — if — if this
21   seems to be something the president's trying to get you to
22   drop it, this seems like a pretty light touch to drop it, to
23   bring it up at that moment the day after he had just fired
24   Flynn to come back in and say I hope we can let this go.
25
26   But then it never reappears again. Did — did it slow down
27   your investigation or any investigation that may or may
28   not be occurring with Michael Flynn?
29
30   **COMEY:** No, although I don't know there're any
31   manifestations — our (sic) manifestations of the
32   investigation between February 14th and when I was fired.
33   So I — I don't know that the president had any way of
34   knowing whether it was effective or not.

1
2 **LANKFORD:** OK. That's fair enough. If — if the president
3 wanted to stop an investigation, how would he do that?
4 Knowing it's an ongoing criminal investigation or
5 counterintelligence investigation.
6
7 Would that be a matter of trying to go to you — you
8 perceive and to say you make it stop because he doesn't
9 have the authority to stop or how — how would the
10 president make an ongoing investigation stop?
11
12 **COMEY:** Again, I'm not a legal scholar. So smarter people
13 answer this better, but I think as a legal matter, president
14 is the head of the executive branch and could direct, in
15 theory, we have important norms against this, but direct
16 that anybody be investigated or anybody not be
17 investigated.
18
19 I think he has the legal authority because all of us
20 ultimately report in the executive branch up to the
21 president.
22
23 **LANKFORD:** OK. Would that be to you, would that be the
24 attorney general? Would that be to who that would do
25 that?
26
27 **COMEY:** Suppose he could do it to — if he wanted to issue
28 a direct order, could do it in any way, could do it through
29 the attorney general or issue it directly to me.
30
31 **LANKFORD:** Well — well, is there any question that the
32 president is not real fond of this investigation? I — I can
33 think of multiple 140 word — character expressions that

1 he's done publicly to express he's not fond of the
2 investigation.
3
4 So I've heard you share before in this conversation that
5 you're trying to keep the agents that are working on it
6 away from any comment the president might have made.
7 Quite frankly, the president has informed around 6 billion
8 people that he's not real fond of this investigation.
9
10 Do you think there's a difference in that?
11
12 **COMEY:** Yes.
13
14 **LANKFORD:** OK.
15
16 **(CROSSTALK)**
17
18 **COMEY:** I think there's a big difference in kicking superior
19 officers out of the Oval Office, looking the FBI director in
20 the eye and saying, "Hope you'll let this go."
21
22 I think if our — if the agents, as good as they are, heard
23 the president of the United States did that...
24
25 **(CROSSTALK)**
26
27 **COMEY:** ... there's a real risk of a chilling effect on their
28 work. That's why we kept it so tight.
29
30 **LANKFORD:** OK. OK. You had mentioned before about
31 some news stories and news accounts, but, without having
32 to go into all the names and the specific times and to be
33 able dip into all that, have there been news accounts
34 about the Russia investigation, about collusion, about this

1 whole event or accusations that, as you read the story, you
2 were stunned about how wrong they got the facts?
3
4 **COMEY:** Yes. There have been many, many stories
5 purportedly based on classified information about — well,
6 about lots of stuff, but especially about Russia, that are
7 just dead wrong.
8
9 **LANKFORD:** I was interested in your comment that you
10 made, as well, that the president said to you, if there were
11 some satellite associates of his that did something wrong,
12 it would be good to find that out.
13
14 That — the president seemed to talk to you specifically on
15 March the 30th and say, I'm frustrated that the word is not
16 getting out that I'm not under investigation, but if there
17 are people that are in my circle that are, let's finish the
18 investigation. Is that how you took it, as well?
19
20 **COMEY:** Yes, sir. Yes.
21
22 **LANKFORD:** And then you made a comment earlier about
23 the attorney general — previous attorney general —
24 asking you about the investigation on the Clinton e-mails,
25 saying that you'd been asked not to call it an
26 "investigation" anymore, but to call it a "matter."
27
28 And you had said that confused you. Can you give us
29 additional details on that?
30
31 **COMEY:** Well, it concerned me, because we were at the
32 point where we had refused to confirm the existence, as
33 we typically do, of an investigation, for months, and it was
34 getting to a place where that looked silly, because the

1 campaigns were talking about interacting with the FBI in
2 the course of our work.
3
4 The — the Clinton campaign, at the time, was using all
5 kind of euphemisms — security review, matters, things like
6 that, for what was going on. We were getting to a place
7 where the attorney general and I were both going to have
8 to testify and talk publicly about. And I wanted to know,
9 was she going to authorize us to confirm we had an
10 investigation?
11
12 And she said, yes, but don't call it that, call it a matter. And
13 I said, why would I do that? And she said, just call it a
14 matter.
15
16 And, again, you look back in hindsight, you think should I
17 have resisted harder? I just said, all right, it isn't worth —
18 this isn't a hill worth dying on and so I just said, OK, the
19 press is going to completely ignore it. And that's what
20 happened.
21
22 When I said, we have opened a matter, they all reported
23 the FBI has an investigation open. And so that concerned
24 me because that language tracked the way the campaign
25 was talking about FBI's work and that's concerning.
26
27 **LANKFORD:** It gave the impression that the campaign was
28 somehow using the same language as the FBI, because you
29 were handed the campaign language and told to be able
30 (sic) to use the campaign language...
31
32 **(CROSSTALK)**
33

1 **COMEY:** Yeah — and — and again, I don't know whether it
2 was intentional or not, but it gave the impression that the
3 attorney general was looking to align the way we talked
4 about our work with the way a political campaign was
5 describing the same activity, which was inaccurate.
6
7 We had a criminal investigation open with — as I said
8 before, the Federal Bureau of Investigation. We had an
9 investigation open at the time, and so that gave me a
10 queasy feeling.
11
12 **LANKFORD:** Thank you.
13
14 **BURR:** Senator Manchin.
15
16 **MANCHIN:** Thank you Mr. Chairman. Thank you, Mr.
17 Comey. I appreciate very much your being here.
18
19 West Virginia is very interested in this — in this hearing
20 that we're having today. I've had over 600 requests for
21 questions to ask you...
22
23 **(LAUGHTER)**
24
25 ... from my fellow West Virginians and most of them have
26 been asked. And there's a quite a few of them that were
27 quite detailed that I'll (sic) ask in our classified hearing.
28
29 I want to thank you, first of all, for coming and agreeing to
30 be here, volunteering. But also volunteering to stay into
31 the classified hearing.
32
33 I don't know if you had a chance to watch our hearing
34 yesterday.

1
2 **COMEY:** I watched part of it, yes, sir.
3
4 **MANCHIN:** And it was quite troubling. My colleagues here
5 at some very pointed questions they wanted answers to.
6 They weren't classified. They could have answered in this
7 open setting. They refused to do so.
8
9 So that even much — makes us much more appreciative of
10 your cooperation.
11
12 Sir, the seriousness of the Russian aggressions in our past
13 elections and knowing that it'll be ongoing as senator King
14 had alluded to, does — what's your concerns there? I
15 mean, what should American public understand?
16
17 **MANCHIN:** People said, "Well, this is a — why are we
18 worried about this? Why make such a big deal out of this
19 Russian investigation?" Can you tell me what your
20 thoughts would be?
21
22 **COMEY:** Yes, sir.
23
24 **MANCHIN:** And then the final thing is on this same topic.
25 Did the president ever˙show any concern or interest or
26 curiosity about what the Russians were doing?
27
28 **COMEY:** Thank you, Senator.
29
30 As I said earlier, I don't remember any conversations with
31 the president about the Russia election interference.
32
33 **MANCHIN:** Did he ever ask you any questions concerning
34 this?

1
2 **COMEY:** Well, there was an initial briefing of our findings,
3 and I think there was conversation there — I don't
4 remember it exactly — where he asked questions about
5 what we had found and what our sources were and what
6 our confidence level was. But after that, I don't remember
7 anything.
8
9 The reason this is such a big deal has — we have this big,
10 messy, wonderful country where we fight with each other
11 all the time, but nobody tells us what to think, what to
12 fight about, what to vote for, except other Americans, and
13 that's wonderful and often painful.
14
15 But we're talking about a foreign government that, using
16 technical intrusion, lots of other methods, tried to shape
17 the way we think, we vote, we act. That is a big deal. And
18 people need to recognize it.
19
20 It's not about Republicans or Democrats. They're coming
21 after America, which I hope we all love equally. They want
22 to undermine our credibility in the face of the world. They
23 think that this great experiment of ours is a threat to
24 them, and so they're going to try to run it down and dirty
25 it up as much as possible.
26
27 That's what this is about. And they will be back, because
28 we remain — as difficult as we can be with each other, we
29 remain that shining city on the hill, and they don't like it.
30
31 **(CROSSTALK)**
32

1 **MANCHIN:** This is extremely important. It's extremely
2 dangerous, what we're — what we're dealing with, and it's
3 needed, is what you're saying.
4
5 **COMEY:** Yes, sir.
6
7 **MANCHIN:** Do you believe there were any tapes or
8 recordings of your conversations with the president?
9
10 **COMEY:** It never occurred to me until the president's
11 tweet. I — I'm not being facetious, I hope there are, and I'll
12 consent to the release of them.
13
14 **(CROSSTALK)**
15
16 **MANCHIN:** So both of you — both of you are in the same
17 findings here — you both hope there's tapes and
18 recordings?
19
20 **COMEY:** Well, I mean, all I can do is hope. The president
21 surely knows whether he taped me, and if he did, my
22 feelings aren't hurt. Release the entire — release all the
23 tapes, I'm good with it.
24
25 **MANCHIN:** Got you. Got you.
26
27 Sir, do you believe that Robert Mueller, the — our new
28 special investigator on Russia, will be thorough and
29 complete, without political intervention? And would you
30 be   confident   (sic)   on   these   findings   and
31 recommendations?
32
33 **COMEY:** Yes. Bob Mueller is one of the finest people and
34 public servants this country's ever produced. He will do it

well. He is a dogged, tough person, and you can have high
confidence that, when it's done, he's turned over all the
rocks.

MANCHIN: You've been asked a wide variety of — of
questions today and we're going to be hearing more, I'm
sure, in our classified hearing. Something I'll often (sic) ask
folks when they come here — what details of this saga
would be — should we be focusing on, and what would
you recommend us do differently? Or to adjust (sic) our
perspective on this?

COMEY: I don't know. I — and one of the reasons that I'm
pleased to be here is I think this committee has shown the
American people, although we have two parties and we
disagree about important things, we can work together
when it involves the core interests of the country.

So I would hope you'll just keep doing what you're doing.
It's — it's good in and of itself, but it's also a model,
especially for kids, that we — we are a functioning, adult
democracy.

MANCHIN: And you also mentioned you had — I think,
what, six — six meetings — three times in person, six on
the phone, nine times (sic) in conversation with the
president. Did he ever, at that time, allude that you were
not performing adequately — ever indicate that at all?

COMEY: No. In fact, the contrary, quite often. Yeah, he
called me one day. I was about to get on a helicopter, the
head of the DEA was waiting in the helicopter for me, and
he just called to check in and tell me I was doing an
awesome job, and wanted to see how I was doing. And I

1 said, "I'm doing fine, sir." And then I finished the call and
2 got on the helicopter.
3
4 **MANCHIN:** Mr. Comey, do you believe you would have
5 been fired if Hillary Clinton had become president?
6
7 **COMEY:** That's a great question. I don't know. I don't
8 know.
9
10 **MANCHIN:** You have any thoughts about it?
11
12 **COMEY:** I might have been. I — I don't know. Look, I — I've
13 said before, that was an extraordinarily difficult and
14 painful time. I think I did what I had to do. I knew it was
15 going to be very bad for me personally, and the
16 consequences of that might have been, if Hillary Clinton
17 was elected, I might have been terminated. I don't know. I
18 really don't.
19
20 **MANCHIN:** My final question will be, after the (sic)
21 February 14th meeting in the Oval Office, you mentioned
22 that you asked Attorney General Sessions to ensure that
23 you were never left alone with the president. Did you ever
24 consider why Attorney General Sessions was not asked to
25 stay in the room?
26
27 **COMEY:** Sure, I did, and — and have. And, in that moment,
28 I...
29
30 **MANCHIN:** You ever talk to him about it?
31
32 **COMEY:** No.
33

1 **MANCHIN:** You never had a discussion with — with Jeff
2 Sessions on this?
3
4 **COMEY:** No, not at all.
5
6 **MANCHIN:** On any of your meetings?
7
8 **COMEY:** No, I don't...
9
10 **(CROSSTALK)**
11
12 **MANCHIN:** Did he inquire — did he — did he show any
13 inquiry whatsoever what was that meeting about?
14
15 **COMEY:** No. You're right, I did say to him — I'd forgotten
16 this — when I talked to him and said, "You have to be
17 between me and the president, and that's incredibly
18 important," and I forget my exact words, I passed along
19 the president's message about the importance of
20 aggressively pursuing leaks of classified information, which
21 is a — a goal I share.
22
23 And I passed that along to — to the attorney general, I
24 think it was the next morning, in our — in a meeting. And
25 — but I did not tell him about the Flynn part.
26
27 **MANCHIN:** Do you believe this will rise to obstruction of
28 justice?
29
30 **COMEY:** I don't know. That — that's Bob Mueller's job to
31 sort that out.
32
33 **MANCHIN:** Thank you, sir.
34

1 Mr. Chairman.

2

3 **BURR:** Senator Cotton.

4

5 **COTTON:** Mr. Comey, you encouraged the president to
6 release the tapes. Will you encourage the Department of
7 Justice or your friend at Columbia or Mr. Mueller to
8 release your memos?

9

10 **COMEY:** Sure.

11

12 **COTTON:** You said that there — you did not record your
13 conversations with President Obama or President Bush in
14 memos. Did you do so with Attorney General Sessions or
15 any other senior member of the Trump Department of
16 Justice?

17

18 **COMEY:** No.

19

20 **COTTON:** Did you...

21

22 **(CROSSTALK) COMEY:** I think it — I'm sorry.

23

24 **COTTON:** ... did you record conversations in memos with
25 Attorney General Lynch or any other senior member of the
26 Obama Department of Justice?

27

28 **COMEY:** No, not that I recall.

29

30 **COTTON:** In your statement for the record, you cite nine
31 private conversations with the president, three meetings
32 and two phone calls. There are four phone calls that are
33 not discussed in your statement for the record. What
34 happened in those phone calls?

1
2 **COMEY:** The president called me, I believe, shortly before
3 he was inaugurated, as a follow-up to our conversation —
4 private conversation on January the 6th. He just wanted to
5 reiterate his rejection of the allegation and talk about —
6 he thought about it more, and why he thought it wasn't
7 true — the — the — the verified — unverified and
8 salacious parts.
9
10 And — and during that call, he asked me again, "Hope
11 you're going to stay, you're doing a a great job." And I told
12 him that I intended to. There was another phone call that I
13 mentioned, I think was — could have the date wrong —
14 March the 1st, where he called just to check in with me as
15 I was about to get on the helicopter.
16
17 **COMEY:** There was a secure call we had about an — an
18 operational matter that was not related to any of this,
19 about something the FBI was working on. He wanted to
20 make sure that I understood how important he thought it
21 was — a totally appropriate call. And then the fourth call
22 — I'm probably forgetting.
23
24 May have been the — I may have meant the call, when he
25 called to invite me to dinner. I'll think about as I'm
26 answering other questions, but I think I got that right.
27
28 **COTTON:** Let's turn our attention to the underlying activity
29 at issue here: Russia's hacking into those e-mails and
30 releasing them, and the allegations of collusion. Do you
31 believe Donald Trump colluded with Russia?
32
33 **COMEY:** That's a question I don't think I should answer in
34 an open setting. As I said, that — we didn't — that (sic)

1 when I left, we did not have an investigation focused on
2 President Trump. But that's a question that'll be answered
3 by the investigation, I think.
4
5 **COTTON:** Let me turn to a couple of statements by one of
6 my colleagues, Senator Feinstein. She was the ranking
7 member on this committee until January, which means she
8 had access to information that only she and Chairman Burr
9 did. She's now the senior Democrat on the — on the
10 Judiciary Committee, meaning she has access to the FBI
11 that most of us don't.
12
13 On May 3rd, on CNN's Wolf Blitzer's show, she was asked,
14 "Do you believe, do you have evidence that there was in
15 fact collusion between Trump associates and Russia during
16 the campaign?"
17
18 She answered, "Not at this time."
19
20 On May 18th, the same show, Mr. Blitzer said, "The last
21 time we spoke, Senator, I asked if you had actually seen
22 any evidence of collusion between the Trump campaign
23 and the Russians, and you said to me, and I'm quoting you
24 now — you said, 'Not at this time.' Has anything changed
25 since we last spoke?"
26
27 Senator Feinstein said, "Well, no. No, it hasn't." Do you
28 have any reason to doubt those statements?
29
30 **COMEY:** I don't doubt that Senator Feinstein was saying
31 what — what she understood. I just don't want to go
32 down that path, first of all, because I'm not in the
33 government anymore, and answering in the negative, I just

1 worry, leads me deeper and deeper into talking about the
2 investigation in an open setting.
3
4 I don't — I — I want to be...
5
6 **(CROSSTALK)**
7
8 **COMEY:** ... I'm always trying to be fair. I don't want to be
9 unfair to President Trump. I'm not trying to suggest, by my
10 answer, something nefarious, but I don't want to get into
11 the business of saying not as to this person, not as to that
12 person.
13
14 **COTTON:** On February 14th, the New York Times published
15 a story, the headline of which was, "Trump Campaign
16 Aides Had Repeated Contacts With Russian Intelligence."
17
18 You were asked earlier if that was an inaccurate story, and
19 you said, in the main. Would it be fair to characterize that
20 story as almost entirely wrong?
21
22 **COMEY:** Yes.
23
24 **COTTON:** Did you have, at the time that story was
25 published, any indication of any contact between Trump
26 people and Russians, intelligence officers, other
27 government officials or close associates of the Russian
28 government?
29
30 **COMEY:** This one, I can't answer, sitting here.
31
32 **COTTON:** We can discuss that in a classified setting, then.
33

1 I want to turn attention now to Mr. Flynn and the
2 allegations of his underlying conduct: to be specific, his
3 alleged interactions with the Russian ambassador on the
4 telephone, and then what he said to senior Trump
5 administration officials and Department of Justice officials.
6
7 I understand there are other issues with Mr. Flynn, related
8 to his receipt of foreign monies or disclosure of potential
9 advocacy activity on behalf of foreign governments. Those
10 are serious and credible allegations that I'm sure will be
11 pursued, but I want to speak specifically about his
12 interactions with the Russian ambassador.
13
14 There was a story on January 23rd in the Washington Post
15 that says — entitled, "FBI reviewed Flynn's calls with
16 Russian ambassador but found nothing illicit." Is this story
17 accurate?
18
19 **COMEY:** I don't want to comment on that, Senator,
20 because I — I'm pretty sure the bureau has not confirmed
21 any interception of communications. And so I don't want
22 to talk about that in an open setting.
23
24 **COTTON:** Would it be improper for an incoming national
25 security adviser to have a conversation with a foreign
26 ambassador?
27
28 **COMEY:** In my — in my experience, no.
29
30 **COTTON:** But you can't confirm or deny that the
31 conversation happened, and we would need to know the
32 contents of that conversation to know if it was, in fact,
33 improper?
34

1 **COMEY:** Yeah, I don't think I can talk about that in an open
2 setting. And again, I've been out of government, now, a
3 month, so I don't — I also don't want to talk about things
4 when it's now somebody's — else's responsibility. But
5 maybe in the — in the classified setting, we can talk more
6 about that.
7
8 **COTTON:** You stated earlier that there wasn't an open
9 investigation of Mr. Flynn in (sic) the FBI. Did you or any
10 FBI agent ever sense that Mr. Flynn attempted to deceive
11 you, or made false statements to an FBI agent?
12
13 **COMEY:** I don't want to go too far. That was the subject of
14 the criminal inquiry.
15
16 **COTTON:** Did you ever come close to closing investigation
17 on Mr. Flynn?
18
19 **COMEY:** I don't think I can talk about that in an open
20 setting, either.
21
22 **COTTON:** I can discuss these more in a closed setting,
23 then.
24
25 Mr. Comey, in — in 2004, you were a part of a well-
26 publicized event about a intelligence program that had
27 been recertified several times, and you were acting
28 attorney general when Attorney General John Ashcroft
29 was incapacitated due to illness. There was a dramatic
30 showdown at the hospital here.
31
32 The next day, you've said that you wrote a letter of
33 resignation, and signed it, before you — went to meet

1 with President Bush to explain why he (sic) refused to
2 certify it. Is that accurate?
3
4 **COMEY:** Yes, I think so.
5
6 **COTTON:** At any time in the three and half months you
7 were the FBI director during the Trump administration, did
8 you ever write and sign a letter of recommendation, and
9 leave it on your desk?
10
11 **COMEY:** Letter of resignation? No, sir.
12
13 **COTTON:** Letter of resignation.
14
15 **COMEY:** No, sir.
16
17 **COTTON:** So despite all of the things that you've testified
18 to here today, you didn't feel this rose to the level of an
19 honest but serious difference of legal opinion between
20 accomplished and skilled lawyers in that 2004 episode?
21
22 **COMEY:** I wouldn't characterize the circumstances of 2004
23 that way. But to answer, no, I — I didn't find — encounter
24 any circumstance that led me to intend to resign, consider
25 to resign. No, sir.
26
27 **COTTON:** Thank you.
28
29 **BURR:** Senator Harris.
30
31 **HARRIS:** Director Comey, I want to thank you. You are now
32 a private citizen, and you are enduring a Senate
33 Intelligence Committee hearing, and each of us get seven

1   minutes instead of five, as yesterday, to ask you questions.
2   So thank you.
3
4   **COMEY:** Now I'm — I'm between opportunities now, so...
5
6   **HARRIS:** Well, you're — you are...
7
8   **(LAUGHTER)**
9
10 ... I'm sure you'll have future opportunities.
11
12 You know, you and I are both former prosecutors. Not
13 going to require you to answer, I just want make a
14 statement that, in — in my — my experience of
15 prosecuting cases, when a robber held a gun to
16 somebody's head, and — and said, "I hope you will give
17 me your wallet," the word "hope" was not the most
18 operative word at that moment. But you don't have to
19 respond to that point.
20
21 I have a series of questions to ask you, and — and they're
22 going to start with, are you aware of any meetings
23 between the Trump administration officials and Russian
24 officials during the campaign that have not been
25 acknowledged by those officials in the White House?
26
27 **COMEY:** That's not a — even if I remember clearly, that's a
28 not a question I can answer in an open setting.
29
30 **HARRIS:** Are you aware of any efforts by Trump campaign
31 officials or associates of the campaign to hide their
32 communications with Russian officials through encrypted
33 communications or other means?
34

1 **COMEY:** I have to give you same answer, Senator.

2

3 **HARRIS:** Sure.

4

5 In the course of the FBI's investigation, did you ever come
6 across anything that suggested that communications,
7 records, documents or other evidence had been
8 destroyed?

9

10 **COMEY:** I think I've got to give you the same answer,
11 because it — it would touch investigative matters.

12

13 **HARRIS:** And are you aware of any efforts or potential
14 efforts to conceal communications between campaign
15 officials and Russian officials?

16

17 **COMEY:** I think I have to give you the same answer,
18 Senator.

19

20 **HARRIS:** Thank you.

21

22 As a former attorney general, I have a series of questions
23 about your connection with the attorney general during
24 the course of your tenure as director.

25

26 What is your understanding of the parameters of General
27 Sessions' recusal from the Russia — Russia investigation?

28

29 **COMEY:** I think it's described in a written release or
30 statement from DOJ, which I don't remember, sitting here,
31 but the gist was he would be recused from all matters
32 relating to Russia and the — and the campaign, or
33 activities of Russia and the '16 election, I think. Something
34 like that.

1
2 **HARRIS:** Is — so is your knowledge of the extent of his
3 recusal based on the public statements he's made? Or
4 the...
5
6 **COMEY:** Correct.
7
8 **HARRIS:** ... OK. So was there any kind of memorandum
9 issued from the attorney general or the Department of
10 Justice to the FBI, outlining the parameters of his recusal?
11
12 **COMEY:** Not that I'm aware of.
13
14 **HARRIS:** And do you know if he reviewed any FBI or DOJ
15 documents pertaining to the investigation before he was
16 recused?
17
18 **COMEY:** I don't. I don't know.
19
20 **HARRIS:** And after he was recused, I'm assuming it's the
21 same answer.
22
23 **COMEY:** Same answer.
24
25 **HARRIS:** And as — aside from any notice or memorandum
26 that was not sent or was, what mechanism or processes
27 were in place to ensure that the attorney general would
28 not have any connection with the investigation, to your
29 knowledge?
30
31 **COMEY:** I don't know for sure. I know that he had
32 consulted with career ethics officials that know how to run
33 a recusal at DOJ, but I don't know what mechanism they
34 set up.

1
2 **HARRIS:** And the attorney general recused himself from
3 the investigation, but do you believe it was appropriate for
4 him to be involved in the firing of the chief investigator of
5 that case — of that Russia interference?
6
7 **COMEY:** That's something I can't answer, sitting here. It —
8 it's a reasonable question, but that would depend on a lot
9 of things I don't know, like what did he know, what was he
10 told, did he realize that the president was doing it because
11 of the Russia investigation — things like that. I just don't
12 know the answer.
13
14 **HARRIS:** You've mentioned in your written testimony and
15 (sic) here that the president essentially asked you for a
16 loyalty pledge. Are you aware of him making the same
17 request of any other members of the Cabinet?
18
19 **COMEY:** I am not.
20
21 **HARRIS:** Do you know one way or another what he...
22
23 **(CROSSTALK)**
24
25 **COMEY:** I don't know one way or another. I never heard
26 anything about it.
27
28 **HARRIS:** And you mentioned that on — you had the
29 conversation where he hoped that you would let the Flynn
30 matter go on February 14th or thereabouts. It's my
31 understanding that Mr. Sessions was recused from any
32 involvement in the investigation about a full two weeks
33 later.
34

1 To your knowledge, was the attorney general — did he
2 have access to information about the investigation in
3 those interim two weeks?
4
5 **COMEY:** I — I don't — I — in theory, sure, because he's the
6 attorney general. I don't know whether he had any contact
7 with any materials related to that.
8
9 **HARRIS:** To your knowledge, was there any directive that
10 he should not have any contact with any information
11 about the Russia investigation between the February 14th
12 date and the day he was ultimately recused — or recused
13 himself, on March 2nd?
14
15 **COMEY:** Not to my knowledge. I don't know one way or
16 another.
17
18 **HARRIS:** And did you speak to the attorney general about
19 the Russia investigation before his recusal?
20
21 **COMEY:** I don't think so, no.
22
23 **HARRIS:** Do you know if anyone in the department, in the
24 FBI, forwarded any documents or information or memos
25 of any sort to the attention of the attorney general before
26 his recusal?
27
28 **COMEY:** I don't — I don't know of any, remember any,
29 sitting here. It's possible, but I — I don't remember any.
30
31 **HARRIS:** Do you know if the attorney general was involved
32 — in fact, involved in any aspect of the Russia investigation
33 after his recusal on the 2nd of March?
34

1 **COMEY:** I don't. I would assume not, but I don't — I don't
2 — let me say it this way. I don't know of any information
3 that would lead me to believe he did something to touch
4 the Russia investigation after the recusal.
5
6 **HARRIS:** In your written testimony, you indicate that you
7 — when you — after you were left alone with the
8 president, you mentioned that it was inappropriate and
9 should never happen again to the attorney general. And,
10 apparently, he did not reply, and you write that he did not
11 reply. What did he do, if anything? Did he just look at you?
12 Was there a pause for a moment? What happened?
13
14 **COMEY:** I — I don't remember real clearly. I — I have a
15 recollection of him just kind of looking at me — and
16 there's a danger here I'm projecting onto him, so this may
17 be a faulty memory — but I kind of got — his body
18 language gave me the sense like, what am I going to do?
19
20 **HARRIS:** Did he shrug?
21
22 **COMEY:** I — I don't remember clearly. I think the reason I
23 have that impression is I have some recollection of almost
24 an imperceptible, like, what am I going to do? But I don't
25 have a clear recollection of that. He didn't say anything.
26
27 **HARRIS:** And, on that same February 14th meeting, you
28 said you understood the president to be requesting that
29 you drop the investigation.
30
31 After that meeting, however, you received two calls from
32 the president — March 30th and April 11th — where the
33 president talked about a cloud over his presidency.
34

1 Has anything you've learned in the months since your
2 February 14th meeting changed your understanding of the
3 president's request? I guess it would be what he has said
4 in public documents or public interviews?
5
6 **COMEY:** Correct.
7
8 **HARRIS:** OK. And is there anything about this investigation
9 that you believe is in any way biased or is — is — is not
10 being informed by a — a process of seeking the truth?
11
12 **COMEY:** No. The — the appointment of a special counsel
13 should offer great — especially given who that person is —
14 great comfort to Americans, no matter what your political
15 affiliation is, that this will be done independently,
16 competently and honestly.
17
18 **HARRIS:** And do you believe that he should have full
19 authority, Mr. Mueller, to be able to pursue that
20 investigation?
21
22 **COMEY:** Yes, and I — and, knowing him well over the
23 years, if there's something that he thinks he needs, he will
24 — he will speak up about it.
25
26 **HARRIS:** Do you believe he should have full
27 independence?
28
29 **COMEY:** Yeah. And he wouldn't be part of it if he wasn't
30 going to get full independence.
31
32 **HARRIS:** Thank you.
33
34 **BURR:** Senator Cornyn.

1
2   **CORNYN:** Thank you, Mr. Chairman.
3
4   Mr. Comey, I'll repeat what I've said at previous hearings,
5   that I believe you're a good and decent man who's been
6   dealt a very difficult hand, starting back with the Clinton e-
7   mail investigation. And I appreciate your willingness to
8   appear here today voluntarily and answer our questions
9   and cooperate with our investigation.
10
11 As a general matter, if an FBI agent has reason to believe
12 that a crime has been committed, do they have a duty to
13 report it?
14
15 **COMEY:** That's a good question. I don't know that there's
16 a legal duty to report it. They certainly have a cultural,
17 ethical duty to report it.
18
19 **CORNYN:** You're unsure whether they would have a legal
20 duty?
21
22 **COMEY:** It's a good question. I've not thought about it (sic)
23 before. I don't know where the legal — there's a statute
24 that prohibits misprision of a felony — knowing of a felony
25 and taking steps to conceal it — but this is a different
26 question.
27
28 And so, look, let me be clear, I would expect any FBI agent
29 who has reason — information about a crime being
30 committed to report it.
31
32 **CORNYN:** Me, too.
33

1   **COMEY:** But where you rest that obligation, I don't know.
2   It exists.
3
4   **CORNYN:** And let me ask you as a general proposition, if
5   you're trying to make an investigation go away, is firing an
6   FBI director a good way to make that happen? By that, I
7   mean...
8
9   **COMEY:** Yeah.
10
11 **CORNYN:** ... doesn't...
12
13 **COMEY:** It doesn't make a lot of sense to me, but I'm —
14 I'm obviously hopelessly biased, given that I was the one
15 fired.
16
17 **(LAUGHTER)**
18
19 **CORNYN:** I understand it's personal.
20
21 **COMEY:** No (sic), given the nature of the FBI, I meant what
22 I said. There's no indispensable people in the world,
23 including at the FBI. That — there's lots of bad things
24 about me not being at the FBI. Most of them are for me.
25 But the work's going to go on as before.
26
27 **CORNYN:** So nothing that's happened that you've testified
28 to here today has impeded the investigation of the FBI or
29 Director Mueller's commitment to get to the bottom of
30 this, from the standpoint of the FBI and the Department of
31 Justice. Would you agree with that?
32

1 **COMEY:** Correct, especially — the appointment of Director
2 — Former Director Mueller is a critical part of that
3 equation.
4
5 **CORNYN:** Let me take you back to the Clinton e-mail
6 investigation. I think you've been cast as a hero or a villain
7 depending on the — whose political ox is being gored at
8 many different times during the course of the Clinton e-
9 mail investigation, and even — even now, perhaps.
10
11 But you clearly were troubled by the conduct of the sitting
12 attorney general, Loretta Lynch, when it came to the
13 Clinton e-mail investigation. You mentioned the
14 characterization that you'd been asked to accept that this
15 was a "matter" and not a criminal investigation, which
16 you've said it — it was.
17
18 There was the matter of President Clinton's meeting on
19 the tarmac with the sitting attorney general, at a time
20 when his wife was subject to a criminal investigation, and
21 you've suggested that perhaps there are other matters
22 that you may be able to share with us later on in a
23 classified setting.
24
25 But it seems to me that you clearly believe that Loretta
26 Lynch, the attorney general, had a — an appearance of a
27 conflict of interest on the Clinton e-mail investigation. Is
28 that correct?
29
30 **COMEY:** I think that's fair. I didn't believe she could
31 credibly decline that investigation — at least, not without
32 grievous damage to the Department of Justice and to the
33 FBI.
34

1 **CORNYN:** And, under Department of Justice and FBI
2 norms, wouldn't it have been appropriate for the attorney
3 general, or, if she had recused herself — which she did not
4 do — for the deputy attorney general to appoint a special
5 counsel?
6
7 That's essentially what's happened now with Director
8 Mueller. Would that have been an appropriate step in the
9 Clinton e-mail investigation, in your opinion?
10
11 **COMEY:** Yes, certainly a possible step. Yes, sir.
12
13 **CORNYN:** And were you aware that Ms. Lynch had been
14 requested numerous times to appoint a special counsel,
15 and had refused?
16
17 **COMEY:** Yes, from — I think Congress had — members of
18 Congress had repeatedly asked. Yes, sir.
19
20 **CORNYN:** Yours truly...
21
22 **COMEY:** OK.
23
24 **CORNYN:** ... did on multiple occasions. And that
25 heightened your concerns about the appearance of a
26 conflict of interest with the Department of Justice, which
27 caused you to make what you have described as an
28 incredibly painful decision to basically take the matter up
29 yourself, and — led to that July press conference.
30
31 **COMEY:** Yes, sir. I can — after the — President Clinton —
32 former President Clinton met on the plane with the
33 attorney general, I considered whether I should call for the
34 appointment of a special counsel, and had decided that

1 that would be an unfair thing to do, because I knew there
2 was no case there.
3
4 We had investigated very, very thoroughly. I know this is a
5 subject of passionate disagreement, but I knew there was
6 no case there. And calling for the appointment of special
7 counsel would be brutally unfair because it would send the
8 message, aha (sic), there's something here.
9
10 That was my judgment. Again, lots of people have
11 different views of it. But that's how I thought about it.
12
13 **CORNYN:** Well, if the special counsel had been appointed,
14 they could've made that determination that there was
15 nothing there and declined to pursue it, right?
16
17 **COMEY:** Sure, but it would've been many months later, or
18 a year later.
19
20 **CORNYN:** Let me just ask you to — given the experience of
21 the Clinton e-mail investigation and what happened there,
22 do you think it's unreasonable for anyone — any president
23 who has been assured on multiple occasions that he's not
24 the subject of an FBI investigation — do you think it's
25 unreasonable for them to want the FBI director to publicly
26 announce that, so that this cloud over his administration
27 would be removed?
28
29 **COMEY:** I think that's a reasonable point of view. The
30 concern would be, obviously, because if that boomerang
31 comes back, it's going to be a very big deal, because there
32 will be a duty to correct.
33

1 **CORNYN:** Well, we — we saw that in the Clinton e-mail
2 investigation, of course.
3
4 **COMEY:** Yes, I recall that.
5
6 **CORNYN:** I know you do. So let me ask you, finally, in the
7 minute that we have left — there was this conversation
8 back and forth about loyalty, and I think we all appreciate
9 the fact that an FBI director is a unique public official in
10 the sense that he's not — he's a political appointee in one
11 sense, but he has a duty of independence to pursue the
12 law pursuant to the — the — the constitutional laws of the
13 United States.
14
15 And so, when the president asked you about loyalty, you
16 got in this back-and-forth about, well, I'll pledge you my
17 honesty. And then it looks like, from what I've read, you
18 agreed upon honest loyalty, or something like that. Is that
19 the characterization?
20
21 **COMEY:** Yes.
22
23 **CORNYN:** Thank you very much.
24
25 **COMEY:** Thank you, sir.
26
27 **BURR:** Senator Reed.
28
29 **REED:** Thank you, Mr. Chairman.
30
31 Thank you, Director Comey.
32
33 There have been press reports that the president, in
34 addition to asking you to drop the Flynn investigation, has

1 asked other senior intelligence officials to take steps which
2 would tend to undermine the investigation into Russia.
3
4 There have been reports that he's asked DNI Coats and
5 Admiral Rogers to make public statements exonerating
6 him or — or taking the pressure off him, and also reports
7 about Admiral Rogers and Director Pompeo — to
8 intervene and reach out to the FBI and ask them.
9
10 Are you aware of any of these, or do you have any
11 information with respect to any of these allegations?
12
13 **COMEY:** I don't. I'm aware of the public reporting, but I
14 had no contact, no conversation with any of those leaders
15 about that subject.
16
17 **REED:** Thank you. You have testified that you interpret the
18 discussion with the president about Flynn as a direction to
19 stop the investigation. Is that correct?
20
21 **COMEY:** Yes.
22
23 **REED:** You've testified that the president asked you to lift
24 the cloud by essentially making public statement that
25 exonerated him and perhaps others. You refused, correct?
26
27 **COMEY:** I didn't — I didn't do it. I didn't refuse the — the
28 president. I told him we would see what we could do, and
29 then the second time he called, I told him, in substance,
30 that's something your lawyer will have to take up with the
31 Justice Department.
32
33 **REED:** All right (sic). And part of the underlying logic was
34 that we've — we've discussed many times throughout this

1 morning — is the duty to correct. That is one of — a
2 theoretical issue, but also a very practical issue. It — was
3 there — your feeling that (sic) the direction of the
4 investigation could in fact include the president?
5
6 **COMEY:** Well, in theory. I mean, as I explained, the
7 concern of one of my senior leader colleagues was, if
8 you're looking at potential coordination between the
9 campaign and Russia, the person at the head of the
10 campaign is the candidate. So, logically, this person
11 argued, the — the candidate's knowledge, understanding,
12 will logically become a part of your inquiry if it proceeds.
13
14 And so I understood that argument. My view was that —
15 that what I said to the president was accurate and fair, and
16 fair to him. I resisted the idea of publicly saying it,
17 although, if the Justice Department had wanted to, that —
18 I would've done it, because of the duty to correct and the
19 slippery slope problem.
20
21 **REED:** And, again, also, you've testified that the president
22 asked you repeatedly to be loyal to him, and you
23 responded you would be honestly loyal, which is, I think,
24 your way of saying, "I'll be honest, and I'll be the head of
25 the FBI and independent." Is that fair?
26
27 **COMEY:** Correct. I tried "honest" first. And also, I mean,
28 you've — see it in my testimony — also tried to explain to
29 him why it's in his interest, and every president's interest,
30 for the FBI to be apart, in a way — because its credibility is
31 important to a president and to the country.
32
33 And so I tried to hold the line, hold the line. It got very
34 awkward, and I then said, "You'll always have honesty

1 from me." He said, "honest loyalty," and then I acceded to
2 that as a way to end this awkwardness.
3
4 **REED:** At the culmination of all these events, you're
5 summarily fired, without any explanation or anything else?
6
7 **COMEY:** Well, there was an explanation. I just don't buy it.
8
9 **REED:** Well, yes. So you're fired. So do you believe that
10 you were fired because you — you refused to — to take
11 the president's direction? Is that the ultimate reason?
12
13 **COMEY:** I don't know for sure. I know I was fired. Again, I
14 take the president's words. I know I was fired because of
15 something about the way I was conducting the Russia
16 investigation was, in some way, putting pressure on him,
17 in some way, irritating him. And he decided to fire me
18 because of that.
19
20 **REED:** Now...
21
22 **COMEY:** I — I can't go farther than that.
23
24 **REED:** ... the Russian investigation, as you have pointed
25 out, and as all my colleagues have reflected, is one of the
26 most serious hostile acts against this country in our
27 history.
28
29 Undermining the very core of our democracy and our
30 elections is not a discrete event. It will likely occur — it's
31 probably being prepared now for '18 and '20 and beyond.
32 And yet the president of the United States fires you
33 because, in your own words — some relation to this
34 investigation.

1
2   And then he shows up in the Oval Office with the Russian
3   foreign minister, first, after classifying you as crazy and a
4   real nut job, which I think you've effectively disproved this
5   morning. He said, "I face great pressure because of Russia.
6   That's taken off." Your conclusion would be that the
7   president, I would think, is downplaying the seriousness of
8   this threat.
9
10 In fact, took specific steps to stop a thorough investigation
11 of the Russian — Russian influence. And also, from what
12 you've said, or what was — been said this morning,
13 doesn't seem particularly interested in these hostile
14 threats by the Russians? Is that fair?
15
16 **COMEY:** I don't know that I can agree to that level of
17 detail. There's no doubt that it's a fair judgment — it's my
18 judgment that I was fired because of the Russia
19 investigation. I was fired, in some way, to change — or the
20 endeavor was to change the way the Russia investigation
21 was being conducted.
22
23 That is a — that is a very big deal, and not just because it
24 involves me. The nature of the FBI and the nature of its
25 work requires that it not be the subject of political
26 consideration.
27
28 And on top of that you have — the Russia investigation
29 itself is vital, because of the threat. And I know I should've
30 said this earlier, but it's obvious — if any Americans were
31 part of helping the Russians do that to us, that is a very big
32 deal. And I'm confident that, if that is the case, Director
33 Mueller will find that evidence.
34

1 **REED:** Finally, the president tweeted that James Comey
2 better hope that there are no tapes of our conversation
3 before he starts leaking to the press. Was that a rather
4 unsubtle attempt to intimidate you from testifying, and
5 intimidate anyone else who seriously crosses his path — of
6 not doing it?
7
8 **COMEY:** I — I'm not going to sit here and try and interpret
9 the president's tweets. It — to me, its major impact was —
10 as I said, occurred to me in the middle of the night — holy
11 cow, there might be tapes. And if there tapes, it's not just
12 my word against his on — on the direction to get rid of the
13 Flynn investigation.
14
15 **REED:** Thank you very much.
16
17 **BURR:** Senator McCain?
18
19 **MCCAIN:** In the case of — Hillary Clinton, you made the
20 statement that there wasn't sufficient evidence to bring a
21 suit against her, although it had been very careless — in
22 their behavior. But you did reach a conclusion in that case
23 that it was not necessary to further pursue her.
24
25 Yet, at the same time, in the case of Mr. Comey, you said
26 that there was not enough information to make a
27 conclusion. Tell me the different between your conclusion
28 as far as former Secretary Clinton is concerned and — and
29 Mr. — Mr. Trump.
30
31 **COMEY:** The Clinton investigation was a completed
32 investigation that the FBI been deeply involved in. And so I
33 had an opportunity to understand all the facts and apply
34 those facts against the law as I understood them. This

investigation was underway, still going when I was fired. So it's nowhere near in the same place. At least, it wasn't when I was...

MCCAIN: But it's still ongoing?

COMEY: ... correct, so far as I know. It was when I left.

MCCAIN: That investigation was going on. This investigation is going on. You reached separate conclusions.

COMEY: No, that one was done. The...

(CROSSTALK)

MCCAIN: That investigation of (sic) any involvement of Secretary Clinton or any of her associates is completed?

COMEY: Yes, as of July the 5th, the FBI completed its investigative work, and that's what I was announcing — what we had done and what we had found.

MCCAIN: Well, at least in the minds of this member, there's a whole lot of questions remaining about what went on, particularly considering the fact that, as you mention, it's a, quote, "big deal" as to what went on during the campaign.

So I'm glad you concluded that part of the investigation, but I — I think that the American people have a whole lot of questions out there, particularly since you just emphasized the role that Russia played.

1 And, obviously, she was a candidate for president at the
2 time, so she was clearly involved in this whole situation
3 where fake news — as you just described it, "big deal,"
4 took place.
5
6 **MCCAIN:** And you're going to have to help me out here. In
7 other words, we're complete — the investigation of
8 anything that former Secretary Clinton had to do with the
9 campaign is over and we don't have to worry about it
10 anymore?
11
12 <u>**COMEY:**</u> With respect to Secretary — I'm not — I'm a little
13 confused, Senator. With respect to Secretary Clinton...
14
15 <u>**MCCAIN:**</u> Yeah.
16
17 <u>**COMEY:**</u> ... we investigated criminal investigation in
18 connection with her use of a personal e-mail server...
19
20 **MCCAIN:** I understand.
21
22 <u>**COMEY:**</u> ... and that's the investigation I announced the
23 conclusion of on July 5th.
24
25 <u>**MCCAIN:**</u> So — but, at the same time, you made the
26 announcement there would be no charges brought against
27 then Secretary Clinton for any activities involved in the
28 Russia involvement in our — engagement in our election.
29
30 I — I don't quite understand how you could be done with
31 that, but not complete — done with the whole
32 investigation of their attempt to affect the outcome of our
33 election.
34

1 **COMEY:** No. I'm sorry, we're not — at least, when I left —
2 when I was fired on May the 9th, there was still an open,
3 active investigation to understand the Russian effort, and
4 whether any Americans work with them.
5
6 **MCCAIN:** But you reached the conclusion that there was
7 no reason to bring charges again Secretary Clinton. So you
8 reached a conclusion.
9
10 In the case of Mr. Comey, you — President Comey (sic)...
11
12 **COMEY:** No, sir.
13
14 **MCCAIN:** ... I mean (sic) — excuse me — case of President
15 Trump, you have an ongoing investigation.
16
17 So you got one candidate who you're done with and
18 another candidate that you have a long way to go. Is that
19 correct?
20
21 **COMEY:** I don't know how far the — the FBI has to go, but
22 yes, that — the Clinton e-mail investigation was
23 completed. The investigation of Russia's efforts in
24 connection with the election, and whether there was any
25 coordination, and, if so, with whom, between Russia and
26 the campaign...
27
28 **(CROSSTALK)**
29
30 **MCCAIN:** You just made it — you just made it...
31
32 **COMEY:** ... was ongoing when I left.
33

1 **MCCAIN:** You just made it clear in what you said, this is a,
2 quote, "big deal," unquote.
3
4 I think it's hard to reconcile, in once case you reach
5 complete conclusion, and the other side, you have — you
6 have not, and you — in fact, obviously, there's a lot there,
7 as — as we know — as you called it a, quote, "big deal."
8 She's one of the candidates. But in her case, you say there
9 will be no charges, and in the case of President Trump,
10 there — the — the investigation continues.
11
12 **MCCAIN:** What has been brought out in this hearing is —
13 is more and more emphasis on the Russian engagement
14 and involvement in this campaign. How serious do you
15 think this was?
16
17 **COMEY:** Very serious. But — I want to say some — be
18 clear. It was — we have not announced, and there was no
19 predication to announce, an investigation of whether the
20 Russians may have coordinated with Secretary Clinton's
21 campaign.
22
23 Secretary Clinton's...
24
25 **(CROSSTALK)**
26
27 **MCCAIN:** ... No, but — they may not have been involved
28 with her campaign. They were involved with the entire
29 presidential campaign, obviously.
30
31 **COMEY:** Of course. Yes, sir. And that is an investigation
32 that began last summer, and, so far as I'm aware,
33 continues.
34

1 **MCCAIN:** So both President Trump and former Candidate
2 Clinton are both involved in the investigation. Yet one of
3 them, you said there's going to be no charges, and the
4 other one, the — the investigation continues.
5
6 Well, I think there's a double standard there, to tell you
7 the truth. Then, when the president said to you — you
8 talked about the April 11th phone call, and he said, quote,
9 "Because I've been very loyal to you, very loyal. We had
10 that thing, you know," did that arouse your curiosity as
11 what, quote, "that thing" was?
12
13 **COMEY:** Yes.
14
15 **MCCAIN:** Why didn't you ask him?
16
17 **COMEY:** It didn't seem to me to be important for the
18 conversation we were having, to understand it. I took it to
19 be some — an effort to — to communicate to me this —
20 that there is a relationship between us where I've been
21 good to you, you should be good to me.
22
23 **MCCAIN:** Yeah, but I — I think it would intensely arouse
24 my curiosity if the president of the United States said "We
25 had that thing, you know" — I'd like to know what the hell
26 that thing is, particularly if I'm the director of the FBI.
27
28 **COMEY:** Yeah, I — I get that, Senator. Honestly, I'll tell you
29 what — this is speculation, but what I concluded at the
30 time is, in his memory, he was searching back to our
31 encounter at the dinner, and was preparing himself to say,
32 "I offered loyalty to you, you promised loyalty to me," and
33 all of a sudden his memory showed him that did not
34 happen, and I think he pulled up short.

1
2 That's just a guess, but I — I — a lot of conversations with
3 humans over the years.
4
5 **MCCAIN:** I think I would have had some curiosity if it had
6 been about me, to be honest with you. So are you aware
7 — anything that would believe you (sic) — to believe that
8 the president or the members of the administration or
9 members of the campaign could potentially be used to
10 coerce or blackmail the administration?
11
12 **COMEY:** That's a subject for investigations, not something
13 I can comment on, sitting here.
14
15 **MCCAIN:** But you've reached that conclusion as far as
16 Secretary Clinton was concerned. But you're not reaching
17 a conclusion as far as this administration is concerned. Are
18 you aware of anything that would lead you to believe that
19 information exists that could coerce members of the
20 administration or blackmail the administration?
21
22 **COMEY:** That's not a question I can answer, Senator.
23
24 **BURR:** Senator's time has expired.
25
26 (UNKNOWN): Thank you.
27
28 **BURR:** All time's expired for the hearing. Can I say, for
29 members — we'll reconvene promptly at 1 p.m. in the
30 hearing room. We have a vote scheduled for 1:45. I would
31 suggest that all members promptly be there at 1 o'clock.
32 We have about three minutes.
33

1 I'd like to have order. Photographers — photographers,
2 return to where you were, please. This hearing's not
3 adjourned yet. Either that, or we'll remove you.
4
5 To members, we have about three minutes of updates
6 that we would love to cover as soon as we get into the
7 closed session, before we have an opportunity to spend
8 some time with Director Comey.
9
10 Based on our agreement, it would be my intentions to
11 adjourn that closed hearing between 2 and 2:10, so that
12 members can go vote, and I would urge you to eat at that
13 time.
14
15 Jim, several of us on this committee have had the
16 opportunity to work with you since you walked in the
17 door. I want to say, personally, on behalf of all this — all
18 the committee members, we're grateful to you for your
19 service to your country, not just in the capacity as FBI
20 director, but as prosecutor, and more importantly, being
21 somebody that loves this country enough to tell it like it is.
22
23 **BURR:** I want to say to your workforce that we're grateful
24 to them — with the level of cooperation that they have
25 shown us, with the trust we've built between both
26 organizations, the Congress and — and the bureau. We
27 couldn't do our job if it wasn't for their willingness to
28 share candidly with us the work that we need to see.
29
30 This hearing's the ninth public hearing this committee has
31 had this year. That is twice the historical year-long average
32 of this committee. I think the vice chairman and my's (sic)
33 biggest challenge, when this investigation has concluded,
34 is to return our hearings to the secrecy of a closed hearing,

1 to encourage our members not to freely talk about
2 intelligence matters publicly and to respect the fact that
3 we have a huge job.
4
5 And that's to represent the entire body of the United
6 States Senate and the American people, to make sure that
7 we work with the intelligence community to provide you
8 the tools to keep America safe, and that you do it within
9 the legal limit, or those limits that are set by the executive
10 branch.
11
12 We could not do it if it wasn't for a trusted partnership
13 that you have been able to lead, and others before you. So
14 as — as we depart from this, this is a pivotal hearing in our
15 investigation. We're grateful to you for the
16 professionalism you've shown, and your willingness.
17
18 I will turn to the vice chairman.
19
20 **WARNER:** I simply want to echo, one, again the thanks for
21 your appearance. And there clearly still remain a number
22 of questions.
23
24 And the one thing I want to commit to you, and more
25 importantly, I think, Chairman, I want to commit to all
26 those who are still potentially watching and following —
27 there's still a lot of unanswered questions, and we're going
28 to get to the bottom of this.
29
30 We're going to get the facts out. The American people
31 deserve to know. There's the questions around
32 implications of Trump officials and the Russians, but
33 there's also the macro issue of what the Russians did and
34 continue to do.

1
2 And I think it is very important that all Americans realize
3 that threat is real. It is continuous. It is not just towards
4 our nation. It is all — towards all Western democracies.
5 And we have to come to a solution set (sic).
6
7 Thank you, Mr. Chairman.
8
9 **BURR:** Director Comey, thank you once again on behalf on
10 the committee.
11
12 This hearing's adjourned.

www.ingramcontent.com/pod-product-compliance
Lightning Source LLC
Chambersburg PA
CBHW071406280526
45787CB00001B/454